Economics is Everywhere

S0-ADF-565

SECOND EDITION

Economics Is Everywhere

SECOND EDITION

DANIEL S. HAMERMESH

University of Texas at Austin

McGraw-Hill
Irwin

Boston   Burr Ridge, IL   Dubuque, IA   Madison, WI   New York
San Francisco   St. Louis   Bangkok   Bogotá   Caracas   Kuala Lumpur
Lisbon   London   Madrid   Mexico City   Milan   Montreal   New Delhi
Santiago   Seoul   Singapore   Sydney   Taipei   Toronto

The McGraw·Hill Companies

McGraw-Hill
Irwin

ECONOMICS IS EVERYWHERE

Published by McGraw-Hill/Irwin, a business unit of The McGraw-Hill Companies, Inc., 1221 Avenue of the Americas, New York, NY, 10020. Copyright © 2006, 2004 by The McGraw-Hill Companies, Inc. All rights reserved. No part of this publication may be reproduced or distributed in any form or by any means, or stored in a database or retrieval system, without the prior written consent of The McGraw-Hill Companies, Inc., including, but not limited to, in any network or other electronic storage or transmission, or broadcast for distance learning.

Some ancillaries, including electronic and print components, may not be available to customers outside the United States.

This book is printed on acid-free paper.

1 2 3 4 5 6 7 8 9 0 DOC/DOC 0 9 8 7 6 5

ISBN 0-07-298260-8

Publisher: *Gary Burke*
Executive sponsoring editor: *Paul Shensa*
Editorial coordinator: *Heila Hubbard*
Senior marketing manager: *Martin D. Quinn*
Lead project manager: *Mary Conzachi*
Lead production supervisor: *Michael R. McCormick*
Design coordinator: *Cara David*
Developer, media technology: *Brian Nacik*
Typeface: *10.5/12 Palatino*
Compositor: *GTS—New Delhi, India Campus*
Printer: *R. R. Donnelley*
Cover art: *Photographer: ©The Solomon R. Guggenheim Foundation, New York Vasily Kandinsky* Upward, *October 1929/Oil on cardboard 27½ × 19¼ (70 × 49 cms). The Solomon R. Guggenheim Foundation, New York, Peggy Guggenheim Collection, Venice, 1976. 76.2553.35*

Library of Congress Cataloging-in-Publication Data

Hamermesh, Daniel S.
    Economics is everywhere/Daniel S. Hamermesh.—2nd ed.
      p. cm.
    Includes index.
    ISBN 0-07-298260-8
    1. Microeconomics. 2. Economics. I. Title.
  HB172.H364 2006
    338.5—dc22   2005041452
www.mhhe.com

Preface

The creation of economic "stories" from real life is an ongoing process, because new stories confront us every day. This new edition contains some of the stories that were generated after publication of the first edition. As with the earlier stories, some of these were inspired by family events, some by news stories, by television shows, movies, music, and other facets of daily life. Some, too, were suggested or corrected by students and colleagues. In this last regard, I would like to thank Peter Debaere, Stephen Donald, Brittani Elliott, Robert Henderson, Ken Hendricks, Joyce Jacobsen, Stephen Lich-Tyler (again), John McGinnis, Robert Mohr, William Todd, Tsu-yu Tsao, Lucille Vaughn, and students at the University of Texas at Austin, the University of Michigan, and the University of New Hampshire. This edition is dedicated to the memory of Morton Hamermesh (1915–2003), who inspired several of the vignettes and who, much more important, inspired much of my professional behavior throughout my career.

Daniel S. Hamermesh

Austin

September 2004

*A*bout the Author

Daniel S. Hamermesh is the Edward Everett Hale Centennial Professor of Economics at the University of Texas at Austin. He received his B.A. from the University of Chicago (1965) and his Ph.D. from Yale University (1969). He taught from 1969 to 1973 at Princeton and from 1973 to 1993 at Michigan State, and he has held visiting professorships at universities in the United States, Europe, Australia, and Asia. He is a Fellow of the Econometric Society, a Research Associate of the National Bureau of Economic Research, Program Director at the Forschungsinstitut zur Zukunft der Arbeit (IZA), and past president of the Society of Labor Economists and of the Midwest Economics Association. He authored *Labor Demand, The Economics of Work and Pay,* and a wide array of articles in labor economics appearing in the leading general and specialized economics journals. His research concentrates on labor demand, time use, and unusual applications of labor economics (to suicide, sleep, and beauty). He has taught introductory microeconomics since 1968 to more than 12,000 students.

*C*ontents

Thinking about Economics Everywhere

In every introductory microeconomics course, you are taught a large number of technical, jargon-type words. These words represent a form of shorthand, a way to summarize ideas about behavior. On the very first day of my introductory class, I teach one word that I believe is the most important of all: *empathy*—the intellectual identification with the feelings, thoughts, or attitudes of someone else. A student should put himself or herself into the particular problem being discussed and ask, "How would I behave if I were confronted with those choices?" Microeconomics is very logical, and most of us think very logically in our daily lives. When confronted with economic questions, though, we too often forget our logic and get scared because somehow the questions seem different. They're not: The economic issues pose the same questions that are posed to us in many of our daily activities and that we almost always answer sensibly and correctly.

The purpose of this book is to illustrate the wide range of daily activities to which an economic way of thinking can be applied. A very few of the roughly 400 vignettes are dated to indicate that they were inspired by something that came up on that particular day, but most arose from more general musing. They are organized according to the topical arrangement of a typical introductory microeconomics course. That way they can tie into what you are learning from any standard introductory textbook. They can focus your ability to apply the formal analysis taught in class to myriad examples that come out of our daily activities. After studying this book, you should be able to see your own activities and the things that you read in newspapers, magazines, and books or hear on television in a new, economic way. As a result, you should be able to understand your world better.

Ideally, you should read and think about the material in this book in small bits at a time—not all at once and not even each chapter at once. Reading and thinking about a few vignettes a day is the best way to learn from this material how to think in economic terms about everyday phenomena. A vignette in Chapter 8 gives good economic reasons why you may not want to do this, but it is the best way to learn from this volume. After reading a vignette, you should go directly to the attached question and try answering it while the thought expressed in the vignette is fresh in your mind.

PART 1

Trade-Offs, Supply, and Demand

CHAPTER 1

Trade-Offs and Opportunity Cost

Production Possibility Frontiers

1.1

Mick Jagger sang, "You can't always get what you want." This is the essence of economics: Wants are unlimited, but the resources to satisfy them are *scarce*. That's true for us as individuals, and it's also true for societies. The same song also states that "if you try sometime you find you get what you need." This statement makes no economic sense. *Needs* is not an economic term. I "need" tickets to the ballet once a week, my private jet with pilot, my home theater, and a chauffeur for the limousine I would like to own. Nobody has the right to argue with my statement about what I "need." Unfortunately, I do not have the income to obtain all these things and, even if I did, the scarcity imposed by the twenty-four-hour day would prevent me from enjoying them in the style I would like. I can satisfy my basic wants; I can afford the time and income for the things that are most important to me. But we all define our needs so broadly that Mick is wrong—you can never get what you need!

> *Q: Make a list of ten things that you "need." Do you get them all? If not, is it because your income isn't high enough or because you haven't got enough time?*

1.2

Forcing us to spend more resources on security (using the National Guard at airports, more checkpoints entering the United States, etc.) is in the end the biggest triumph by terrorists. The government pays National Guard troops and, since the guards-people are not at their regular jobs, output outside the security sector is diminished. The output of the security people doesn't give us anything that we would want if there were no perceived need for security. The resources used for this purpose are like a negative change in technology; they shift the **production possibility frontier** inward. In this case, unlike in the example of Mick Jagger's singing, our behavior implies that our desire for security is a basic need—it comes before anything else.

Q: Is this vignette correct? After all, the security guards get paid and buy things, so aren't they adding to output?

1.3

The six- and four-year-old grandchildren were in my office play-ing with my Razor Scooter. Each would get on the scooter, ride it to the other end of the hall, then ride it back to my office. Each took a round-trip, then gave it to the other, turn after turn; each spent time getting off, handing the scooter to the other. After a while, the six-year-old said, "Why don't you take three turns, then I'll take three turns?" His younger sister agreed, and they played happily thereafter, each taking three roundtrips, then let-ting the other have the scooter. This freed up wasted time, getting the kids to an efficient point, one on the **production possibility frontier** for the rides they were taking.

Q: You have drawn production possibility frontiers in class. How would you draw what happens to the production possibility frontier in the case outlined in this vignette?

1.4

A great example of **trade-offs** comes from the life of a full-time student. Such students can be imagined as having only two uses of their time—studying and socializing—and two outputs from those uses—knowledge acquired and social satisfaction. If a stu-dent is efficient, he or she cannot increase the amount of knowl-edge acquired in college without giving up social satisfaction. The **opportunity cost** of one more unit of social satisfaction is some amount of forgone knowledge, and the opportunity cost of another unit of knowledge is forgone social satisfaction. This **production possibility frontier** can shift out along each axis.

A speed-reading course moves the curve out along the axis for knowledge acquisition, allowing the student to obtain *both* more knowledge and more social satisfaction (because some time that can be saved from studying can be shifted to socializing). It's harder to think of improvements that move the curve out along the social satisfaction axis. One regrettably out-of-date example is the "Orgasmatron" in Woody Allen's movie *Sleeper*.

Q: Draw the production possibility frontier implied in this vignette. List one other example of a technical improvement that shifts the frontier out the learning axis, and one other that shifts it out the social satisfaction axis.

1.5

When you consider the student's trade-off between socializing and learning, it is possible to think of examples that would represent technological improvements in each of these "industries" separately (as Vignette 1.4 shows). In class, I just couldn't come up with an improvement that would raise productivity in both activities—that would shift the **production possibility frontier** out along both axes. A student volunteered "strip-studying" in the Adam Sandler movie *Billy Madison* as an example. That seems like a pretty good one—essentially this change allows the student to combine learning and (some form of) socializing in the same time period. It makes each minute of a student's time more productive (in terms of the two goals of learning and "socializing").

Q: The production possibility frontier implied in this vignette is the same as the one you started off with in the question above. Now list one other example of a technical improvement that shifts the frontier out along both axes.

1.6

A constant complaint by longer-term residents (more than one year) in rapidly growing Austin, Texas, is that the city is "too crowded." People complain about the traffic, crowded parks and swimming holes, and so on. They never complain about the growth in the number and variety of restaurants, theaters, and cultural events or about the increase in specialized retail outlets in town. The two are related: Bigger cities bring broader and more diverse culture and activities. The **trade-off** is that they also bring more crowds and traffic congestion. New people, those who made the choice to accept the crowds in exchange for more excitement, are clearly better off. Longer-term residents may indeed be worse off because they chose to come to the area when the trade-off was different. Some of them may have benefited from the trade-off: They may like the greater breadth of activities more than they dislike the added congestion. Other longer-term residents, though, may be worse off: The change in the trade-off goes against the preferences that initially drew them to Austin.

*Q: Graph the **production possibility frontier** implied by this discussion, labeling the axes carefully. [Hint: One "good" might be speed and ease of access to stores, theaters, malls, and so on.] How would that frontier shift if a new invention allowed everyone to move around town twice as fast?*

1.7

Most of the techno-toys we buy—computers, PDAs, and the like—make us better off (otherwise we wouldn't buy them). Most also involve a **trade-off** between cost and convenience: They save time and improve our lives, but they cost more to buy than the items they replaced. Very few such toys both make us better off *and* reduce our total dollar expenditure. This was true even for such techno-toys of the 1940s and 1950s as automatic washers and dryers and TVs. One is my cell phone. Because night and weekend minutes are essentially free, now that we're using the cell phone for long-distance calls, our regular phone bill has fallen by more than the monthly cost of the cell phone plan.

Q: Name technical improvements in your life that have actually reduced the dollars you spend on the general activities that the improvements are part of.

1.8

Many students believe that professors are either good researchers or good teachers, but not both. This belief implies that there is a negative relationship between research and teaching comparing across different professors. I don't believe this is true at all: The better researchers are also the better teachers. This doesn't mean that professors have no **trade-offs** in their activities. Instead, those who are good at one thing are good at the other, and those who are mediocre at one are typically mediocre at both. There is a trade-off for each individual, but the overall level of ability differs among professors so that some professors can perform better in both areas.

> *Q: Draw the production possibility curves for a high-ability professor and a low-ability professor that are implied by this vignette. Label the axes carefully.*

1.9

With the death of so many old people in France in the recent heat wave, the French government is under pressure to do more for the elderly (a group that will be growing in importance in the population of that country over the next few decades). One proposal is to ask the entire French workforce to give up one holiday a year. The extra tax revenue gained would be earmarked for programs for the elderly. Essentially the government is proposing a **trade-off**—asking society's working members to sacrifice now so that today's elderly, and today's workers too when they get older, will have more. Like every trade-off, this means that something must be given up (leisure today) in order to gain something (benefits for old people today and in the future). You can't have both the leisure and the benefits.

> *Q: This is an example of a nation giving up leisure today in order to have more in the future. As a student, what are the examples in your own life where you give up leisure today in order to have something in the future that you wouldn't otherwise have obtained?*

1.10

A student e-mailed an interesting question: "You spent all the time in class talking about technical progress and how it shifts the **production possibility frontier** outward. Has there ever been a case of technical regression that shifted it inward?" If there were a nuclear disaster and we actually lost technology (forgot how to manufacture chips, lost the art of internal combustion, etc.), it would make sense to characterize this as a reduction in technology. (Of course, if we fell back that far, there probably wouldn't be people teaching the idea of production possibility frontiers in colleges and universities!) The only real-life example might be the loss of certain technologies that the Romans developed—indoor plumbing and a few others—that were not rediscovered until after the 1600s at least. That would be the best, although very outdated, example of a technological regression.

Q: Technical regression for a society is extremely rare. Cases where a household sees an inward shift in what it can produce are more common. List some things that might cause such an inward shift to occur for a single household.

Opportunity Cost

1.11

September 8, 2003—Last night, President Bush said the United States will do "whatever is necessary" in Iraq. This is a standard line of political rhetoric, and it sounds good. But is it likely to be true? And does it really make any economic sense? If "whatever is necessary" costs $1 trillion per year, I doubt that the American people want to sacrifice 10 percent of the goods and services they produce in order to solve the mess in Iraq (or any other foreign country, for that matter); and I doubt Mr. Bush would have been reelected if he went ahead and spent these resources. Like everything else in politics and economics, there is a **trade-off** here—the additional resources proposed for spending in Iraq have a positive **opportunity cost.**

*Q: The Iraq war cost around $100 billion in its first year, roughly 1 percent of all goods and services produced in the United States in a year. Does this spending represent waste—a movement inside a **production possibility frontier?** Or does it represent a redefinition of a frontier, with a new "good" being produced?*

1.12

In the movie *The Hand That Rocks the Cradle*, a female character comments that "today's woman has to do three things: bring home at least $50,000 per year . . . and cook homemade lasagna." It is unlikely that many women will be able to do all three, because the first and third are probably **substitutes.** A woman who is earning that much money is unlikely to have the time to cook homemade lasagna because there is a **scarcity** of time, her most important resource. The opposite side of the coin is that a woman who has chosen to spend time rolling homemade pasta is unlikely to have enough time to earn this much. (The second thing [. . .] probably can be done by both high-earning women and those who have chosen to stay at home.) But fixed resources—twenty-four hours in the day—diminish the likelihood that most women will be able to do all three things.

> *Q: Are the **opportunity costs** of earning and cooking constant over the day and the week, or can women (and men too) find times when one is relatively cheap and the other is relatively costly? What are these times?*

1.13

One of my female colleagues commented on the previous entry, stating, "I earn more than $50,000, and I also make homemade lasagna." My response was that **production possibility frontiers** differ, depending on a person's or country's resources and technology. She is very efficient at many things and can both earn a lot and make great home-cooked lasagna. Nonetheless, even she faces a **trade-off,** assuming that she is working and enjoying leisure efficiently. If she works more, she can earn more, but she will have less time for home cooking. If she cooks more, she won't be able to earn so much.

> *Q: Draw her production possibility frontier in these two activities. Now draw a point that accounts for the fact that she spends one hour a day doing absolutely nothing.*

1.14

The local newspaper has a story about how different public universities rank in the percentage of lower-division courses that are taught by tenure-stream faculty (as opposed to temporary faculty or graduate teaching assistants). The University of Texas at Austin has 46 percent of lower-division credit-hours taught by faculty. Why not 100 percent? The answer is clear: Faculty resources are scarce, and the **opportunity cost** of a faculty member teaching a lower-division class is one less upper-division or graduate-level class taught. The university could have 100 percent of its lower-division classes taught by tenure-stream faculty; but then upper-division classes would be fewer in number, and they would have more students per class. The problem is that faculty teaching resources are scarce.

> Q: What are your preferences—would you rather have more regular faculty in your introductory class? What will your attitude be when you are a senior? How about when you are an alumnus or alumna?

1.15

September 13, 2001—My wife and I donate more than $100 for relief for the September 11, 2001, New York terrorist attack. Our five-year-old grandson offers to give $1 of his savings to help out. We have a much higher income than our grandson; in fact, he doesn't earn a penny, relying only on a tiny allowance from his parents. Who is sacrificing more? Whose **opportunity cost** of the contribution is greater—our grandson's or ours?

> Q: Does the fact that our grandson and we are responding to the request for contributions after September 11 make our opportunity cost any different from what it would be if the charitable request were, for example, for the local United Way?

1.16

At a party recently, one of my colleagues mentioned that his fourteen-year-old daughter was babysitting for her six- and three-year-old siblings so that her parents could be at the party. I asked how much they were paying the teenager, and he answered that she was being paid nothing. He noted, however, that if his wife and he wanted the daughter to babysit, but she was called by someone else to babysit for pay, they would match the market rate that she would have received outside the house. My colleague is paying the girl **opportunity cost.** When she has an alternative babysitting job that pays, she receives a rate of pay at home equal to her opportunity cost—what she was offered for babysitting elsewhere. When she has no alternative job, she is again paid the opportunity cost of her time—which is then zero! Only an economist would do something like this.

> Q: If you were in the daughter's position, would you settle for what you would be paid elsewhere? Are there economic reasons why you might be willing to settle for less, or to insist on—and get—your parents to pay more than others would pay for your babysitting services?

1.17

The main function of the College of Liberal Arts Promotion and Tenure Committee is to discuss granting lifetime tenure to faculty members at the end of their probationary periods (typically six years). The dean of the college, a professor of Sanskrit, asked the following question: "Could we do better hiring a person from outside the university in place of the person we are considering for promotion? After all, we are granting someone a salary of at least $60,000 a year for the remainder of his or her career." The **opportunity cost** of granting a lifetime job to a professor is the benefits that could be obtained from an alternative use of the salary the professor would be paid over his or her lifetime.

> *Q: Let's say the typical professor earns $60,000 per year. What is the opportunity cost of granting lifetime tenure to a thirty-five-year-old professor who will work until age seventy?*

1.18

A student told me that she bought a "Hook 'em Horns" souvenir cap through eBay (for her boyfriend, who goes to Texas A&M). She paid $10. Why are people spending time selling very low-value items on eBay? Surely the amount they earn from these sales cannot justify the time spent setting up the auction; the hourly wage they make has got to be below any reasonable estimate of the **opportunity cost** of their time. A lot of the eBay material is sold there because of the novelty of running one's own auction and the fun of playing on the Web this way. eBay auctions are at least in part consumption for both sellers and buyers.

> *Q: Perhaps the vignette misses the point by focusing on **trade-offs** at a single point in time. Might spending your time using eBay now be a method of learning that allows you to be much more efficient when you want to auction other, more valuable items in the future?*

1.19

Opportunity Cost and the "Terrible Twos." Our two-year-old granddaughter typically gets read to and put to bed by her mom, while her dad reads to and puts her older brother to bed. Last night, the parents switched, and the little girl cried until her mom reverted to her usual role. Tonight, her mom was away for the evening, and so her dad read to her. She sniffled a bit initially, then looked around and realized there was no alternative—her mom wasn't there. She calmed down, understanding even at age two that when the **opportunity cost** is very high, one needs to be satisfied with an otherwise less desirable alternative (in this case, her father).

> *Q: Can you put a dollar figure on the opportunity cost here? If not, does that mean that the concept is useless in this case? Give two other examples where you can't measure opportunity cost, although you believe the concept is relevant.*

1.20

The editor's comment in *Celebrated Living*, American Airlines' quarterly luxury magazine, is, "[Our] covers have featured some of the world's most high-profile celebrities, including Michael Jordan, Robert Redford, Clint Eastwood, Giorgio Armani, and Claudia Schiffer. In each interview, these fascinating people all singled out the same thing as the ultimate luxury: time." This is no doubt true for them: They all have enough income to buy all the goods and services they could want. Their "problem" is that, like you and me, they have only twenty-four hours a day to consume those goods. They can hire people to do things for them, buy Jaguars instead of Chevrolets, and still not spend all their income or have enough time to enjoy all the things they have bought. Their **opportunity cost** of time is very high in part because they could earn a huge amount if they worked. It is also high because they have an abundance of goods to consume, but no more time to spend consuming them than anyone else does.

> *Q: What would you do if you magically had two more hours per day? How would you spend the extra time? How would the things you buy change as a result of this time windfall?*

1.21

Service at our local post office is incredibly slow. On a normal day, fifteen or twenty minutes may go by as we wait to mail a package or buy stamps. During the Christmas rush weeks, the wait is typically a half hour or more. Last week, a Mailboxes, Etc.

store opened up in the vacant space next door to the post office. What a great location decision! The post office is in a small strip mall. A coffee shop that had recently occupied the space was one of several stores that went bankrupt in quick succession, illustrating the relatively low **opportunity cost** of the space. While apparently low in value for alternative uses, such as coffee shops, the space is quite valuable when used by a commercial mailer. I got tired of waiting in line at the post office, went next door, and in two minutes mailed my packages. I was willing to spend more money, and less of my valuable time, to accomplish the task of mailing out seasonal gifts. The clerk said that they had gotten a lot of business from people who saw the long lines at the post office and chose to save time by using their commercial services. My guess is that most of those people had jobs, and fairly high-paying ones at that.

Q: What are two other examples where a potential business location has a low opportunity cost except in a particular specialized use that is made valuable because of something next door or in the neighborhood?

1.22

Each semester, after course grades were sent out, I used to be deluged with phone calls and e-mail from students asking why they got the grades they did (always below what they expected). The answer usually was that they messed up on the final exam. A late colleague suggested a way of reducing this harassment. He pointed out that the students' **opportunity cost** is low after exam week and stays low until classes start the next semester. To discourage students from calling and e-mailing, he said that he writes on the exam that no complaints about grades will be acknowledged until the second week of the next semester. At that time, students' opportunity cost of time is higher: They have better things to do, including attending their new classes. Only students who are deeply bothered by what they thought was unfair grading are willing to incur the high cost of inquiring. His suggestion has succeeded in sharply reducing the number of inquiries I receive.

Q: How does this policy treat students differently by year in school (freshman, sophomore, etc.), by the number of courses they are taking, and in other ways?

1.23

March 2003—A story in yesterday's newspaper talked about the increasing **opportunity cost** of spending more soldiers' time in Afghanistan hunting for Osama bin Laden. Army Special Operations leaders are trying to determine whether the search is the best use of the limited resources of the soldiers in the most elite units. One Special Operations colonel suggested that the opportunity cost of searching for Osama is the value the soldiers might have in hunting for terrorists elsewhere. Perhaps, too, the elite forces' opportunity cost might increase with an attack on Iraq.

Q: Assume there is no other American war going on, and that the only military use of the Special Operations forces is searching for Osama. What is the opportunity cost of their time?

CHAPTER 2

Demand and Supply Curves

Demand

2.1

On a cold January day when our older son was five years old, he came into the house with an ice-covered rock, probably a small piece of cement. He asked me, "Daddy, would you buy this for ten cents?" I said no, that was too much money for this particular rock. He then said, "Maybe you'll buy it for five cents." I said yes. Even though the rock was really ugly, I was pleased that our five-year-old son understood that **demand curves** slope downward and was willing to cut his price to sell his product.

> *Q: Offer to sell a much younger sibling, cousin, niece, or nephew ballpoint pens or CDs that you think might interest him or her. Start off with a high price and then work your way down. (This is like what we call a Dutch auction.) See if you can trace out the equivalent of a downward-sloping demand curve.*

2.2

Another bad night's sleep! Perhaps that's because my wage is too high. Sleep takes time, and time has value—its **opportunity cost.** Instead of sleeping, I could be working and earning a wage. A study of the economics of sleep a number of years ago showed that higher-wage people sleep less. Your wage is the price of sleep, and there is a downward-sloping **demand curve** for sleep. The demand curve shifts with other characteristics: Having young kids at home reduces the amount of sleep people get, especially women. Additional nonwage income—inheritances and gifts—has small positive effects on sleep time, and people say that if they had more hours in the day, extra sleep is one of the top three things they would do with that extra time. Because time is scarce (there will always be only twenty-four hours in a day), the amount we sleep requires economic decision making.

> *Q: If your long-lost relative suddenly left you $1 million, would you sleep more or less? If somehow you were granted an extra two hours per day, how much extra per day would you sleep? What else would you do with the two hours?*

2.3

We lived in the North all our lives and used to love to go to the Caribbean in the winter. Since moving to Texas nine years ago, we have not gone at all. Today, an old friend from the North suggested a reunion with other old friends in the Virgin Islands next December. We'd like to see all of these friends, but we have no real interest in going to the Caribbean. Have our tastes for Caribbean vacations changed, thus shifting our **demand curve?** *No!* The good being demanded is not Caribbean vacations but rather the pleasure of being in a warm climate. We get that pleasure every winter living in Texas, so why travel 2,000 miles for still more of it? Tastes don't change in most cases if we properly define the good that is being demanded.

> *Q: Assume you believe that Caribbean vacations combine two goods: pleasure from warm weather and gorgeous beaches. What happens to the demand for a Caribbean vacation by someone living in Texas if the vacation combines both of these goods?*

2.4

How do you decide which movies to pay to see, which books to read, and so forth? What shapes our **demand curves** for very particular products? The decisions depend on tastes, but partly also on the information you acquire about the movies or books. The problem is deciding what source of information to use. There are too many reviews and too many friends offering advice to pay attention to them all. Typically, we acquire the information from people we trust, people whose past recommendations have proved valuable. I listen to movie reviewers who have done well for me in the past. This creates tremendous inertia: It's hard for a new reviewer or friend's comments to affect my thinking. Only if I'm suddenly short of advice might I spend the time paying attention to a new reviewer and perhaps listening to his or her advice. It's also hard to ditch familiar reviewers who've done well in the past, but it does happen. For years, we chose movies on the basis of (the late) Siskel and Ebert recommendations. One New Year's Eve, we went to a movie that Ebert claimed was the best of the year, *Breaking the Waves*. This painfully boring piece lasted three and a half hours, totally spoiling our evening. Since then, we have paid no attention to Ebert's recommendations: With the big shock of his disastrous recommendation, he moved out of the group of information providers whom we spend our scarce time paying attention to when we make our choices.

Q: Who is likely to exhibit more inertia in using information about movies, books, and so on, someone age eighteen or someone age fifty-eight? Give an economic reason for your answer.

2.5

During a stay in Russia in 1993, my wife and I went to the Maryinsky Theater in Saint Petersburg, where many of the most well-known ballets in the repertoire premiered. Among them is *Swan Lake*, which was playing on a Thursday night. We went to the theater, bargained for tickets outside the theater just before the show, and got great seats for only $7.50 per seat. On Saturday night, we went back and decided to bargain for tickets to see *Legends of Love*, not a major work. The best price we could get was $20 per seat, barely low enough to persuade us to see the ballet. Why the difference? There were very few tourists early that June, and Russian workers typically don't go out much during the week. On Saturday, Russians were competing for the tickets along with the few tourists. What shifted the **demand curve** wasn't what was playing, but when it was showing.

*Q: If you were planning programs for the Maryinsky Theater and wanted to get the most **revenue** for the theater, would you put the popular ballets on weekdays, as in this case, or the mediocre ones?*

2.6

The arrest of Allan Iverson, star basketball player and spokesperson for Reebok, raised questions about whether Reebok's sales would be hurt. Does a corporate symbol's infamy *increase or decrease the demand* for the products of the company that he or she advertises for? On the opposite side of the coin, do Lance Armstrong's six consecutive victories in the Tour de France help sales of U.S. postage stamps (since he wears the colors of the U.S. Postal Service cycling team)? The answer probably depends on both the nature of the product and the publicity surrounding the star-symbol. One doubts whether Americans, who hardly follow competitive cycling, will buy more stamps because of Lance Armstrong; and Europeans, who love cycling, are unlikely to buy American postage stamps regardless. Iverson's negative publicity might actually have increased Reebok's demand in the short run by getting the company's name in the news; in the longer run, though, it may be negative, as most people associate sporting goods such as shoes with a more wholesome image than is projected by a guy accused of assaulting his wife.

> *Q: Assume you are the marketing manager for a brand of building blocks. Would you be willing to pay a sports figure to endorse your product? How about if you were marketing manager for a salve that eases the itching from athlete's foot? How and why do your answers differ?*

2.7

A news story mentioned the fact that the percentage of people cremated in the United States rose from 3 percent to nearly 30 percent in the last quarter century. A spokesperson for the funeral directors association attributed this tremendous increase to the increased mobility of the American population: If you live far away from Grandpa and will not be visiting his grave, why not put him in an urn instead of in the ground? Does the rapid growth of cremation represent a shift in demand, as the spokesperson implies? Or does it instead represent people's substituting away from a product (burials) that has risen rapidly in price? It's difficult to tell: The quantity (of cremations) transacted can shift both because the demand has increased and because the price of its close **substitutes** has risen a lot. It is worth noting that no industry spokesperson is ever going to claim that a shift has occurred because consumers have responded to relative changes in price—to the rising price of burials. These people always argue that some factor beyond the industry members' control caused the change. Price matters, but businesses don't want consumers to be reminded of that *except* when a business cuts prices.

> *Q: If funeral directors got together and agreed to raise the price of a cremation to equal that of a burial, how would that affect the demand curve for cremations?*

2.8

A rerun of *Law and Order* involved gang warfare in Manhattan. A New Jersey gang had been encroaching on the turf of a Manhattan gang's drug-selling operation. A number of murder victims had been found: people who did not seem like gang members. The victims turned out to be former customers of the Manhattan gang who had begun buying from the New Jersey gang. The murders were designed to scare other customers away from buying from the New Jerseyites and back to buying from the Manhattan gang—to shift **demand curves** in the two markets. If you can't advertise your product publicly, one way to encourage customers to buy from you instead of from your competitors is by convincing them that the price of buying from the competitor might be death. A murder threat adds greatly to the price of a product and probably has a profound effect on consumers' demand.

> *Q: What else might shift a consumer's demand curve for drugs sold by a particular gang?*

2.9

According to Roman legend, a series of prophecies by the god Apollo were written down in nine books and interpreted by the Sibyl of Cumae (an old woman living in a cave whose interpretations were sought on numerous occasions by Roman leaders). Around 500 BC, the Sibyl gave the Roman king Tarquinius Superbus a chance to buy the books for a price payable in gold. He refused. According to myth, the Sibyl burned three of the books and offered the king the remaining six for the original price she had asked for the nine. He refused again; she burned three more books and offered him the remaining three at the same price she had asked for all nine. This time he paid her. Why would he do that? How can his behavior be seen as consistent with the theory of consumer demand? By reducing the number of books in existence, the Sibyl

made it clear to him that the remaining ones were now *scarcer.* She
changed the quality of the product in the king's mind, which induced him to pay a price three times higher per book than he would
have paid if he had bought the books at the original price.

> *Q: Are there other examples where sellers destroy some of their
> product in order to enhance the value of what remains by so much
> as to increase their total **revenue?** Why don't we see very many
> other sellers behaving like the Sibyl and trying to convince people
> how valuable their product is by throwing some of it away?*

2.10

Environmental and other groups are running advertisements
reminding people who buy SUVs that the large amounts of gasoline they buy may help finance terrorism—the argument being that
some of the revenues go to countries that condone terrorist acts.
The ads' purpose is to shift the **demand curve** for gasoline leftward
by getting people to reduce demand for its **complement,** the SUV.
I'd be really surprised if this ad campaign works—it's pretty far-
fetched—but it does point out the possible relationships among the
three activities: SUV use, gasoline consumption, and terrorism.

> *Q: If the advertising campaign were to be successful, graph how
> it would affect the markets for SUVs and gasoline.*

2.11

On the *Tonight Show,* Jay Leno mentioned that a plastic surgeon in
Los Angeles was offering a discount on breast implants for
Mother's Day. This doesn't seem to make any economic sense:
Nobody will give this present to his or her mother, and Mother's
Day is hardly associated with this surgical procedure. The holiday may be only an advertising convenience. The issue is more
likely that **demand curves** shift to the left in the late springtime.
People do not want to have cosmetic surgery that will inhibit
them from walking around with little clothing, and the swimsuit
season is almost here. By offering a discount, the surgeon can
keep his office busy at a time when the quantity transacted would
otherwise be low.

> *Q: If this interpretation of the advertisement is correct, what
> other medical specialties would you expect to offer seasonal dis-
> counts, and why?*

2.12

Relative to other professional occupations, the pay of elementary and secondary teachers in the United States has fallen over the past 50 years. The decline has been especially true for women, since women's pay economywide in the United States has risen relative to men's. A recent study examined how this relative decline has affected the quality of women entering K–12 teaching. Over the past half-century, women in the top 10 percent of measures like SAT scores have shown a sharp decline in their presence in teaching. Their opportunities in other occupations have increased as sex segregation has diminished, and they have moved down the **supply curve** to teaching as its relative pay has fallen. The average quality has fallen only slightly—the biggest drop has been among the very most able women, those whose opportunities outside of teaching have increased most rapidly.

> *Q: This vignette talks about the supply of high-quality women workers to precollege teaching. There has, in fact, been a huge increase in the number of women teaching in colleges and universities. What does that tell you about the pay that they receive compared to their alternatives?*

Supply

2.13

One of the students, a Russian émigré, tells me he left Russia to avoid being drafted into the army. I mentioned that I had heard young men can bribe someone for $100 and avoid being drafted. He said that's true, but for a bribe as low as $100 the exemption from service is offered by a low-level bureaucrat; and that exemption may not be honored by the people who decide whether you are drafted or not. To guarantee that you escape from the army, you need to bribe a high-level official whose exemption will be respected by everyone. That costs thousands of dollars. Apparently, the **supply curve** of exemptions from the army is upward sloping in the price—the bribe that must be paid.

> *Q: You are driving in a poor country, are stopped on a traffic violation, and clearly discern that the policeman would like a bribe. Would the bribe cost you more or less than in a similar situation in a richer country?*

2.14

I took my watch in to have the battery replaced. The jewelry store clerk said they could do it but would not be able to have it back until two days later. They could not do it any faster. Indeed, that seems to be very common: There are not that many activities in which things can be speeded up if you pay more. Why not? Surely for a higher price stores would be willing to provide services more rapidly, to let you get ahead in the "line" if you are willing to pay more. The **supply curve** should slope upward.

> *Q: List some reasons why the speeded-up market is not available. How would the supply–demand situation in the market for speeded-up service be different if I lived in a small town? An extremely big city?*

2.15

Even gangsters' **supply curves** slope upward. In his book *But He Was Good to His Mother* (Jerusalem: Gefen, 2000), Robert Rockaway reports that an associate of Big Jack, a New York gangster in the early twentieth century, stated to police that Big Jack had the following price list for his services: slash on cheek with knife, $1 to $5; shot in leg, $1 to $25; shot in arm, $5 to $25; throwing a bomb, $5 to $50; murder, $10 to $100. Clearly, the prices are higher for the more difficult tasks; and the range of prices for a particular criminal act probably reflects the ease of access to the target. Perhaps a shot in the leg costs less than one in the arm because hitting a person in the leg without causing further damage is easier than hitting someone in the arm.

> *Q: Draw a supply curve for criminal activities. Then show how it would shift if unemployment were low and there were many good legitimate jobs. Then show how the curve would shift if jobs were scarce.*

2.16

In the movie *Catch Me If You Can*, Leonardo DiCaprio winds up in a hotel room (in the 1960s) with a woman he discovers is a very high-priced call girl. She says, "You can have me for the night—just say the right price." He says "$300," and she throws a card at him and says, "Go fish!" He then says $500, getting the same answer, then $600, with the same result. He finally says $1,000, and she agrees. As with most activities, this transaction, too, has an upward-sloping **supply curve.**

Q: Is $600 the opportunity cost of the call girl's time? Is $1,000? What does this story tell you about her opportunity cost?

2.17

The rental market at the New Jersey shore this summer is depressed. Prices have dropped, and owners who used to require people to rent for a full month now are willing to rent for only two weeks at a time; some even offer one-week rentals. The reason has to do with extremely low interest rates last summer. These low rates induced a lot of people to buy houses along the shore last year, since the mortgage costs were low and thus the total cost of buying dropped. This meant that this summer the owners, who seldom occupy the housing during the summer, have put these additional potential rental properties on the market at the shore. That *increase in supply* of rental properties has made it easier for us to find the perfect place to take our annual beach vacation.

Q: What will this relative glut in vacation rentals do to the amount of time that the property owners spend at the shore themselves this summer?

Which Curve Shifts?

2.18

Johnson and Johnson (J&J), the giant pharmaceutical company, is running television ads promoting nursing as a rewarding career (and has even created a Web site, www.discovernursing.com). This would seem like a charitable public-service campaign, but I'm skeptical. If it is successful, the ad campaign will induce more people to enter nursing, reducing the nursing shortage and/or lowering nurses' equilibrium wages. Along with nursing and other services, J&J's drug products make up the cost of medical care; they are **complements** in producing medical care. If one input becomes cheaper, costs and eventually the price of medical services fall. That fall in turn generates a rise in the amount of medical care demanded. It may be cynical, but J&J's apparently

altruistic action can be viewed as an indirect way of raising the amount of its own product that is demanded.

> *Q: Graph **supply** and **demand curves** in the markets for nurses and J&J products before and after J&J undertakes its successful advertising campaign.*

2.19

The 2004 Summer Olympic Games were held in Athens, Greece. The Greek government expected that the games would bring a huge influx of tourists, spectators, journalists, and athletes to Athens. Because of this temporary boom in the population, the government also expected a big *increase in demand* for prostitutes. To meet this increased demand in a country where prostitution is legal, Greek authorities proposed opening 30 new legalized brothels in the Athens area. Their efforts represent a movement along the **supply curve** that has been generated by the shift in demand.

> *Q: What about the market for souvenir sellers—would the same story apply to them, too, or is there something different about the market in this vignette?*

2.20

One of the silly things our grandchildren do each year at the beach is try to catch seagulls. This year, I asked the seven-year-old what he would do if he caught one. He said, "I would sell it for $20." I asked him what if nobody would buy it at that price, and he responded, "Then I would sell it for $1." Clearly, seven-year-olds understand the **law of demand.** Now the grandchildren have never caught a seagull and almost surely never will, but we were talking about how to catch one. My eighty-seven-year-old father told his great-grandchildren, "Lie flat and still on the beach, put some seagull food on your belly, and grab the seagull when he comes to eat it." It doesn't seem possible to increase the number of seagulls supplied by offering them more food—moving up along the **supply curve**—as there is always lots of seagull food on the beach. Dad's scheme to shift the supply curve of seagulls to the right thus seems the best way for the grandchildren to get more seagulls—or at least catch one.

> *Q: Would my Dad's scheme work better or worse if there were less garbage on the beach?*

CHAPTER 3

Demand and Supply Together—Quantity and Price in Unrestricted Markets

Single Markets

3.1

Teaching a class of 500 students introductory microeconomics is hurting my voice, and I've had to cut back on my cigar smoking. I am only one of many cigar smokers. But what if all Americans found out that cigar smoking hurts their voices? What would happen to the **equilibrium price** and **equilibrium quantity** in the cigar market in the United States? What would happen to the Cuban economy (some people do have access to illegal Cuban cigars)?

> *Q: Draw the supply–demand graphs implied by this vignette and trace the effects of the behavior that is implied. Then show in the graph what would happen in all the markets discussed here if the opposite occurred and the surgeon general announced, "Cigar smoking reduces cancer and is generally beneficial for health."*

3.2

One of the students in my class is a saxophone player. Like all reed-instrument players, he buys a lot of reeds for his instrument. In 2001, bamboo trees in a large part of the world were infected with a virus that destroyed much of the bamboo crop. This change shifted the **supply curve** of bamboo to the left. This shift raised the price of bamboo, which is the major input into making reeds. As a result of this increase in the input price, the supply curve of reeds shifted leftward, too. The student noticed that the price of reeds skyrocketed. Being a smart young fellow, he wisely *decreased the amount of reeds he demanded* each month because they now were more expensive. He moved leftward along his **demand curve** for reeds.

> *Q: As anyone who lives in a warm climate (like Central Texas) knows, bamboo is a weed that grows quite rapidly. How long do you think it will be until the original equilibrium in this market is restored?*

3.3

There have been stories all over the Web and on television in the last few weeks about the low-carbohydrate food craze—people following weight-loss diets that involve sharp reductions in their intake of carbohydrates. One story on Yahoo said, "Food companies rush to take advantage of carbohydrate crunch." This is a good description of behavior in a market where the **demand curve** has shifted to the right. The demand shift is due to people's new belief that these diets will enable them to lose weight. To meet the shift in demand—and seeing a chance to make additional profits—food companies are happy to produce more low-carbohydrate foods. They are happy to *increase the amount supplied* in response to the shift in demand.

> *Q: What does this change in consumer behavior do to the equilibrium price of low-carbohydrate foods?*

3.4

In the James Bond movie *Goldfinger*, the main character, Auric Goldfinger, owns a huge horde of gold. The plot centers on his attempt to explode a nuclear device at Fort Knox, where the U.S. gold supply was housed at that time. He hatches this plot in order to irradiate the U.S. gold supply, rendering it valueless. His idea is that with the U.S. gold horde gone, the world **equilibrium price** of gold will rise. His wealth, which consists of the value of the gold he owns, will increase with no additional effort on his part.

> *Q: Analyze in a supply–demand graph the economics of Goldfinger's activities. What would happen in the market if after Goldfinger's success people decided that gold rings were not necessary mutual gifts to brides and grooms? [Extra credit, not economics: How long before the nuclear device was scheduled to explode did James Bond shut down its timer?]*

3.5

There is an active market in smuggling Somali children into Europe and North America. Given poor economic conditions and poor economic prospects for their children in Somalia, Somali parents are willing to pay to give their children a better future in the industrialized world (and perhaps eventually to send remittances back to their parents). The parents have a demand curve for smuggling their children out of the country, and a substantial supply of smugglers has grown up to meet the demand. Before the September 11 terror attacks on the United States, the market price for smuggling a Somali child to New York or Washington was $3,500. Afterwards, the price doubled to $7,000. This is not surprising—the **supply curve** shifted leftward. More careful border guarding and immigration controls made the smuggler's job more difficult, essentially increasing the quantity of an input, smuggler's time, needed to get one Somali child safely into a Western country.

> *Q: Draw the graph depicting the situation in this market before and after September 11, being careful to indicate who are the suppliers and who are the buyers. Then draw what would happen in the market if there were a very serious drought in Somalia.*

3.6

A story in the local newspaper reported on the 17 percent salary increase (to $1.7 million per year) that our football coach is getting. The story went on to talk about the tremendous explosion in the salaries of head football coaches in NCAA Division I universities in the last several years. This has occurred even though **revenues** generated from college football have shown no obvious increase. The reason for the boom is that the market for

professional football head coaches has increasingly become inte-
grated with the college market, with a number of college coaches
moving to the National Football League (NFL) (e.g., Spurrier to
the Redskins for $5 million per year) and vice versa. Salaries in
pro football are now spilling over into college football. College
football has always been a subsidized training program for pro
football, and now the coaching markets are becoming more inte-
grated as well.

> *Q: Show what would happen to the market for college coaches if
> the NCAA allowed schools to pay salaries to the college athletes
> they are training to play in the National Football League. What
> would happen to this market if people got tired of watching college
> football on television and instead spent more time watching the
> NFL on television?*

3.7

The headline in the local newspaper reads, "Central Texas had
nation's widest gap between supply and demand [of office space]
in '01." A graph in the story shows occupancy rates falling from
97 percent to 86 percent during the year. Another graph shows
that the rental price per square foot had risen from $12 in 1991 to
$26 in 2000, as this area boomed, but had fallen to $24 in 2001.
The problem will be heightened, so the story states, by the com-
pletion this year of one million square feet of additional office
space—an outward shift in the **supply curve** at a time when the
demand curve has shifted inward. If I were planning to rent
office space and seeking bargains, I'd wait a few months.

> *Q: Given the state of this market, what would you do if you were
> leasing office space? What would you do if you were one of the peo-
> ple who had a new office building that could be completed in the
> next three months? What would you do if you had already dug a
> hole to build an office building but had not gone any further?*

3.8

If free to do so, markets tend toward an **equilibrium** where
supply equals demand. That's even true for the market for
dating, as shown in the 1960s No. 1 hit song, "Surf City," by Jan
and Dean. They sing, "We're going to Surf City; gonna have
some fun . . . Two girls for every boy." Two girls for every boy is

not an equilibrium—it is a disequilibrium situation. There is a **shortage** of boys and a **surplus** of girls. Jan and Dean are going to Surf City, having been attracted by the surplus of girls. Their arrival there will reduce the size of the surplus of girls and also reduce the shortage of boys. If enough other boys follow their lead, the market for dates in Surf City will be in equilibrium—the shortage and surplus will have been removed by the action of the market as people respond to the shortage of boys by "going to Surf City."

> *Q: If you have ever been to a mixer or a singles bar where there is an excess of members of one sex, why did this excess arise? What prevented the equilibrium, roughly equal numbers of men and women, from being reached?*

3.9

At lunch we were talking about the fact that female porn stars are paid many times what male porn stars are paid. On the supply side, the ability to fake a good performance is clearly greater for women than for men, and that should make women's pay lower. Also on the supply side, though, the number of men willing to enter this occupation may exceed the number of women. Clearly, supply is much less important than demand: The clientele consists almost exclusively of men who want to look at women and are willing to pay large premiums for what they view as attractive women. Most of the audience has little interest in looking at the men on the screen, and the men's wages reflect that.

> *Q: In his novel* The Wanting Seed, *Anthony Burgess described a world in which homosexuality was encouraged and was much more common than heterosexuality. In such a world, there would presumably still be pornography. How would the supply–demand situation and the relative wages of male and female porn stars be different compared to what they are in today's market?*

3.10

A book I'm reading describes the reaction to Gutenberg's invention of the printing press in the 1450s by noting, "Professional copyists opposed it, . . . along with aristocrats who feared that their libraries would decrease in value" (Stuart Isacoff, *Temperament,*

New York: Knopf, 2001). It's nice to see that even in the fifteenth century people understood the impact of increases in supply on the wages of workers producing a **substitute** and on the **equilibrium price** in the market. It also makes one thankful for progress: We did not see huge protests from the producers of mechanical calculators when they were displaced by electronic ones or computers in the 1960s and 1970s or from watchmakers and watch repairers when quartz watches became popular at around the same time.

> *Q: Graph the market for copyists' services in the fifteenth century and show the impact of the invention of the printing press. Think of two other innovations that had similar effects in the market for workers with particular skills.*

3.11

A story in the *New York Times* discussed a problem in London: a shortage of taxis on the streets in the evening and at night. The problem is not an overall shortage of London cabs, but that drivers don't want to work evenings and nights. The solution: The city government raised the regulated rates for evening–night cab fares to about 30 percent above daytime fares. This has encouraged a 20 percent increase in the number of drivers who are willing to switch from day work. Is this increase big enough? The fare increase will reduce the number of cab trips demanded, too. Unless the shortage was immense—more than 20 percent excess demand—we can expect the initial large increase in the supply of cabbies to be excessive. Passengers should have no trouble finding cabs, and cabbies will be complaining about insufficient demand.

> *Q: Graph the situation in this market before and after the nighttime fares were raised. Show the new price in relation to the equilibrium in this market if the new fare is too high.*

3.12

Washington, D.C., has a $1 surcharge for downtown taxi rides during rush hour. This is somewhat like the previous vignette, but different: This is a fixed dollar amount; that was a percentage surcharge. As with the London surcharge, the purpose is to *increase the amount supplied* (in Washington, during a time of peak demand). Why is the surcharge a fixed amount in Washington and a percentage in London when the purposes are so similar? The reason is that fares in Washington are also fixed: You pay the same amount for any taxi ride within the downtown zone, no matter what the distance. In London, the fare is metered by distance. At first glance the surcharges appear to create different incentives, but coupled with each town's basic pricing structure, they create similar incentives. Both function as percentage increases in taxi fares.

*Q: As a result of this surcharge in rush hours, what will happen to the **equilibrium price** and equilibrium quantity for taxi rides outside rush hours?*

3.13

March 16, 2002—Only six months after the September 11 terrorist attacks, there's a truly depressing sight in U.S. airports: American flag paraphernalia is now discounted heavily. (In the local airport a sign reads, "All patriotic T-shirts now $4.99.") Have Americans already forgotten those recent events? I doubt it, although the initial explosion of demand for these souvenirs has passed. Suppliers, eager to meet what they saw was a tremendous shortage of patriotic clothing, geared up production lines and increased the *amount supplied* to meet the huge *increase in demand.* Some of them overshot the mark, leading to temporary surpluses once the initial increase in demand had been satisfied.

Q: By April 21, the same place was advertising, "All patriotic T-shirts now $2.99." Does this change surprise you?

3.14

A story in today's local newspaper about declining personal computer (PC) prices states, "As a general rule, the supply of parts needed to build computers exceeds the demand, and prices decline steadily. Steady improvements in performance also push down prices for existing technology." These sentences are garbled economics. It's true that PC prices have declined steadily. That's not because supply always exceeds demand, but instead because technical improvements keep shifting **supply curves** outward, reflecting firms' ability to offer PCs profitably at lower prices. It's not a matter of continual disequilibrium, but instead that the **equilibrium price** keeps changing as technology improves. Also, how could "steady improvements in performance" be compatible with "existing technology"? They're not; the story is again describing the process of technological improvements driving down input (parts) costs and steadily *increasing the supply* of PCs.

> *Q: Draw the **supply** and **demand curves** in the market for computer parts. Show how these curves have shifted over time, carefully indicating what has happened to the equilibrium price and quantity sold.*

3.15

The general manager of WDIV-TV in Detroit editorialized on air this week about rising gasoline prices. He was particularly annoyed that gas prices seem to rise around holiday weekends. I would be very unhappy if they didn't rise then. Demand is high on those weekends, and the storage capacity of gasoline stations is limited. If prices didn't rise, the amount demanded would be even higher, and we would observe temporary shortages of gasoline and a lot of unhappy drivers. The high price around holidays is what keeps supply and demand in balance.

> *Q: Graph the unrestricted equilibrium in the market for gasoline before a holiday. Then show what would happen if gas station owners listened to the general manager and held the price constant in response to the shock of a holiday weekend.*

3.16

Airlines have had frequent-flyer programs for over twenty years. The stock of unredeemed frequent-flyer mileage is like consumer income. It is used in the market for a limited number of seats to "buy" "free tickets" on the airline. The amount of unredeemed mileage has more than doubled in the last five years, while the "price" of a seat—25,000 miles on American Airlines, for example—has not changed. During the recession, the market demand for paid airline tickets was low, and the airlines kept the supply of seats set aside for free tickets unchanged and did not alter the "price." As the economy recovered, the **demand curve** by paying customers shifted outward, and airlines maximized profits by reducing the supply of free seats to frequent flyers. At that time, a shortage began to exist in the market for free seats. Holders of mileage found it increasingly difficult to obtain tickets for travel at the times they wanted; not surprisingly, in response to this the airlines raised the price of a free ticket to equilibrate the rising demand and the reduced supply.

Q: Draw the market for free seats before the growth in unredeemed mileage. Then show how that growth has shifted demand in that market. Then show the market during and after the recession.

Related Markets

3.17

A story in *The Economist* points out, "Wool production in Australia has hit record lows, sending prices to a 15-year high." Clearly, this is a leftward shift in the **supply curve.** It is probably caused by the long drought in Australia that has reduced the ability of Australian sheep to produce as large fleeces as before. The sharp rise in wool prices has had an effect on a related market—that for cotton. The same story reports that the price of cotton, which recently had been at a three-decade low, increased 50 percent in the last year. This is not surprising. Cotton and wool are **substitutes,** and the rising price in the wool market has caused producers to shift more to cotton for apparel, thus increasing the demand for cotton.

Q: Draw the implications of this vignette for the wool market, and then for the cotton market.

3.18

An advertisement for financial advice in the *Toronto Globe and Mail* shows a naked couple in bed making love. (This ad probably would not appear in an American newspaper.) Below the picture is a small banner with a stylized news report saying, "Sheer Inc. recalls 100,000 condoms." On the right side of the picture are three graphs: The first shows the stock price of Sheer Inc. falling as it moves out the x axis over time. The second shows the stock price of Cupid Condom Inc., presumably a **substitute** for Sheer Inc., rising as it moves out the x axis. The final graph shows sales of maternity wear, also substitutes for condoms, rising as they move out the x axis.

> *Q: If you were drawing up a revision of this advertisement, what two extra graphs depicting additional markets would you put on the right side of the picture? In other words, what are some other related goods that would also be affected by the Sheer Inc. recall?*

3.19

The biggest hits in the literary world right now are Hillary Clinton's autobiography and the new Harry Potter book, which came out a few days after Senator Clinton's book and was kept under lock and key prior to midnight on its publication date. A shipment of 7,500 copies of the Harry Potter book was stolen, and nobody could identify the thief. On the *Tonight Show*, Jay Leno mentioned this, then "identified" the thief—Hillary Clinton! If this were true (it is not), it makes good sense: In a pair of related markets, which well might be the case if people are going to read only one popular book, Harry Potter and Senator Clinton's biography are **substitutes.** One might imagine that Hillary Clinton wishes to reduce the number of available copies of the Harry Potter book in order to induce book buyers who can't buy what they want to purchase her book instead.

> *Q: Draw supply–demand graphs of the market for Hillary Clinton's memoir and for the Harry Potter book, and show what happens in each if someone destroys some of the Harry Potter books.*

3.20

The U.S. government subsidizes cattle grazers to use federally owned lands (mostly in the West). The average price per month per animal unit is around $1.50. Private landowners charge around $11 per month per animal unit on their lands; the free-market price is around $11 per month. Does that mean that the **subsidy** is $9.50 per month? *No*—it's more than that. The federal subsidy induces cattle grazers to use federal lands. That shifts their demand away from private lands. The federal subsidy lowers the **equilibrium price** on private lands below what would prevail if there were no subsidy. In an unsubsidized market, demand for grazing private lands would be higher, resulting in an equilibrium price above $11.

> *Q: Graph the market **supply** and **demand curves** for grazing on federal and private lands. Show the effect of the subsidy to grazing on federal lands on the prices observed in each market, and then show what would happen if the subsidy were removed.*

3.21

For many years, there has been a brisk trade in the genitalia of harp seals and hooded seals, as well as in reindeer antlers. These unusual products are sold to men in Asia as aphrodisiacs. A study in *Environmental Conservation* shows that the quantity of harp seals slaughtered in Canada fell from 250,000 per year before 1998 to less than 100,000 per year afterward. Yet the price of seal genitalia also fell, from $70 per item beforehand to $20 afterwards. Clearly, the **demand curve** for these aphrodisiacs shifted leftward. Why? The most likely answer is that many of the former customers have been switching to a more potent substitute good—Viagra. This substitute was unavailable before 1998 (its price was infinity) but is now available and affordable. Its lower price has reduced the demand for the related natural substitutes, the animal by-products.

> *Q: Graph the market for seal genitalia before and after the introduction of Viagra.*

3.22

We're going to Moscow this December day. Reading the guidebook, my wife is concerned about pickpockets and muggers. I point out that it's so cold that there has been a seasonal *decrease in supply* of pickpocket targets—tourists like her. In the cold weather, people's wallets are not easily accessible to professional pickpockets. She is not reassured by my comments. She points out that, with the reduction in supply in the pickpocket market, there will be an *increase in demand* from mugging as pickpockets shift to the mugging market. So long as pickpockets can transfer their skills to mugging—so long as these markets are related—she is correct in not being reassured.

> *Q: Draw the market for pickpocketing in Moscow, and show what happens to the equilibrium in the cold weather. Then draw the effects on the market for muggings in Moscow.*

3.23

When asked "Why rob banks?" Willie Sutton, a famous bank robber of the 1920s and 1930s, answered, "Because that's where the money is." In the movie *3,000 Miles to Graceland*, Kurt Russell's character leads a gang of Elvis impersonators who are planning to rob a casino. When asked "Why rob the casino?" he answers, "Because everyone else robs banks." His answer implies that he believes that the market for robbing banks is overcrowded, and that the returns to robbing yet another bank are likely to be small. Robbing casinos is a natural **supply** response to the low returns in the overcrowded **related market** for robbing banks.

> *Q: Draw the market for robbing casinos. What happens in this market if the Las Vegas police, who have become aware of the shift of robbers from banks to casinos, redirect their crime prevention more toward casinos?*

3.24

Walking through the lobby of the San Diego Marriott Hotel, I see an empty wall with a bunch of chairs in front of it. The wall seems to have contained a bank of pay telephones, and these have apparently been carefully removed. Pay telephones are a **substitute** for cell phones. With the growth of cell phone use, the **demand** for pay phones has surely dropped greatly. But why remove the phones? After all, they have already been set up, so they cannot be generating much further cost; and removing them costs money. In fact, there are substantial **opportunity costs** if the unused pay phones are left intact. First, each pay phone has a telephone number; and the growth of cell phones, fax lines, and so on, has made phone numbers a scarce resource. (Witness the proliferation of area code designations needed to accommodate the explosive use of communication devices.) Second, the space taken up by the bank of pay phones has some potential alternative uses—perhaps with chairs as an area for guests to converse, or for a cart selling muffins and coffee—that would enhance the value of the hotel. Removing the severely underutilized phones is a wise business decision.

> *Q: Lots of pay phones are still found in airports and other places. Where would you expect to see pay phones still in place, and from what kinds of places would you expect to see them removed? Why?*

3.25

Every Saturday in a Jewish synagogue, a section out of the Five Books of Moses is read. The next weekend, the portion includes Genesis 41:1–36, dealing with Joseph's interpretation of Pharaoh's dream, where Joseph tells Pharaoh to set aside one-fifth of the produce in the good years to tide the country over during the upcoming famine. This is a classic example of **speculation:** shifting supply from a time when supply is high to a time when it is low. The question is: Why one-fifth? Why not more or less? Presumably, Joseph had some idea of how much of the stored grain would deteriorate, how bad the famine would be, and how the Pharaoh valued the current consumption of his subjects compared to their future consumption. He must have chosen one-fifth by accounting for all these factors, since he was a pretty smart fellow.

> *Q: Graph the supply–demand situations in the good years and the bad years. Then show how Joseph's suggestion affects the markets in the two different times. Now show how the amount Joseph asked the Pharaoh to set aside will change if Joseph believed that a plague of rats might infest the stored grain. How would it change if Joseph believed that Egypt would have an influx of foreign purchasers (like his brothers) during the time of famine? Graph both cases.*

CHAPTER 4

Demand and Supply— Quantity and Price in Restricted Markets

Price Ceilings

4.1

Congressman Howard P. "Buck" McKeon (Republican of California) proposed putting a **price ceiling** on tuition at public colleges and universities. He would limit the amount that they could increase tuition from one year to the next. Should students be cheering him on? How would his bill, if enacted, affect higher education in the United States? Current students will probably benefit—their tuition in their remaining few years in college will probably rise less rapidly than otherwise. But the bill would also prevent colleges from funding the kinds of quality programs that many students now and in the future might want. Also, better professors will seek jobs in colleges, private ones mainly, that can afford to pay for their services; and public universities won't be able to maintain facilities as well as in the past. This is really a bill that is designed to make public higher education in the United States more mediocre.

> *Q: If you are at a public institution of higher learning, find out how much of its total costs are covered by students' tuition. Calculate how much less funding the college would have if tuition were decreased by 1 percent per year (which would be the effect, after inflation, of this price ceiling). Ask your econ professor how that funding might affect teaching/research in economics in your school.*

4.2

Several years ago, Cambridge, Massachusetts, was forced by a statewide referendum to end its rent control program. Rent controls are a **price ceiling** on apartment rentals. Their removal created a free market for the over one-third of the Cambridge housing stock whose rents had been controlled. Not surprisingly, rental prices rose very rapidly. Owners had not been making repairs to their housing, but freeing up the rents generated a boom in investment in improving the housing stock: Building permits increased 50 percent. Removing the restrictions on this market produced exactly the results that economic thinking would predict: higher prices, but higher quality, too. Since the city relies on property taxes, freeing up the housing market also generated an increase in property tax funds flowing into the city's coffers.

Q: Draw a supply–demand graph describing the Cambridge housing market before and after the removal of rent controls.

4.3

The Cirque du Soleil show "O" is a permanent installation in the Bellagio Hotel in Las Vegas and is in tremendous demand. The highest face price for a ticket is $125, but they are unobtainable; the free-market (scalpers') price is $250, far above the **price ceiling** of $125. Tickets are also allocated outside the free market— a certain number are bought by the major casinos very early and are given away "for free" to the casino's high rollers. For these people, the price of the ticket is not zero, though: The dollar price is zero, but these people generate enough extra profits for the casino, since the average player loses money gambling, so that the total price to the higher rollers is probably at least $250.

Q: Why doesn't the casino just charge $250 per ticket? Why doesn't it charge the high rollers $250 and take a little bit smaller profit on each gamble?

4.4

Dead People Help You Get Gasoline. The African nation of Zimbabwe is currently an economic mess, with, among other things, **price ceilings** on gasoline leading to **shortages** and long lines at the gas stations. The government has set up priorities for obtaining gasoline, with hearses being priority recipients. Two mortuary workers were arrested for leasing out bodies to motorists, who would take the body to a gas station, claim the hearse's priority to obtain the gasoline, then return the body to the mortuary to be leased out again. The motorist would then siphon out the purchased gasoline for use in his own private vehicle. This is a natural response of the market to circumventing the shortages. The government created the shortage—and the opportunity for someone to profit from it—and the market responded.

Q: Siphoning gasoline is dangerous—poisoning or explosions are possible. Why would anyone accept these risks? Why engage in this method of circumventing the price ceiling?

4.5

We exchanged our excellent second-row center mezzanine seats to the opera tomorrow night for seats tonight at the same price but higher up and way off to one side. Why were these seats priced the same? How does the opera company decide which season ticket holder gets the better seats within each section? It would be too complicated to charge large numbers of different prices depending on individual rows, center or side, and so on. The costs of administering that system would be too great. Instead, there are only a few prices, none of which represents the single **equilibrium price,** with customers allocated within the section partly based on first-come, first-served, and partly based on the size (if any) of each customer's money contribution to the opera company. The contribution functions as an additional price that removes the disequilibrium resulting from the small number of different prices. This kind of pricing is widespread: For fifteen years, we had tickets on the five-yard line, high upper deck, for the Michigan State University football season. We never moved closer to the fifty-yard line or farther down. Big Ten rules and the same administrative costs that caused the opera company's behavior prevented the athletic department from charging different prices in the faculty section. It was well known that generous contributions guaranteed better seats.

Q: Student seats at college football games are allocated by lottery at many schools. Why don't the schools allocate the better student seats the same way as seats for the faculty, by giving better seats to students who contribute to the athletic program?

4.6

At my favorite southwestern cuisine restaurant, the prices of entrees are much higher than they were a year ago. At 6:30 PM, there were still some empty tables. In past years, the place was completely packed and a long line was already forming by 6:15 PM. I pointed out to a colleague how sensitive people's demand to price is, even in the case of good restaurant meals. He asked, "Are you sure it's that, or has the *demand* shifted because of the recession?" Good point—a decline in quantity sold could result from either cause. Merely observing that there has been a reduction in the equilibrium quantity doesn't tell us whether we are moving up a **demand curve** or whether the demand has shifted left. I don't know, but in this case I think I'm right. If the recession were the cause, why would the restaurant have gone ahead and raised prices? The higher prices reflect a decision to seek a less price-conscious clientele: to raise **revenue** by moving up a nearly vertical demand curve. Unsurprisingly, this was the first time at this restaurant that the management was happy to let the customers linger over dinner.

> *Q:* *Would the restaurant management have been more or less likely to raise prices if, instead of a recession, the area had been in an economic boom? In that case, would the management have been as willing to let customers eat a leisurely dinner?*

4.7

March Madness—The NCAA basketball tournament usually offers great examples of economic behavior, since tickets to the games (especially the final sixteen matches) are sold in markets with tremendous excess **demand.** The Midwest Regional in 2000 was held in Michigan, where ticket scalping is illegal. Worse still, the police were serious about enforcing the antiscalping ordinances. Ticket scalpers got around the police and the restrictions in a very clever way. If you wanted to buy the best ticket available, you could buy it from a scalper at the same price he or she paid, but you also were forced to buy a map of the arena to show you where the seat was, and the map was priced at $1,000! This equilibrated the market—the full price of the ticket, including the outrageously priced map, was just enough to eliminate any excess demand.

> *Q: Have you ever bought a ticket for a sporting event or concert for more than the face value of the ticket? Would it have made any difference to you if you had been charged the same amount but part of the total cost was for a map, some popcorn, two "free drinks," or something else?*

4.8

Places at Czech universities are limited; the **supply curve** is vertical. Rather than charging tuition for this scarce good, the universities base admission on competitive exams. The entrance exams include tests on Czech history and language. Because the universities are quite good by eastern European standards, many Russian high school students would like to attend. In the United States, these "out-of-state" students would be allowed in, but would pay very high tuition. Charging tuition isn't possible in the Czech Republic. Instead, lucrative businesses have arisen that offer training in the Czech language and history to foreign students seeking to do well on the entrance exams and be admitted to Czech universities. Even though the universities create a **shortage** of places by keeping tuition low, the market has created a product—the entry training courses—that essentially functions as part of the price foreigners pay to go to Czech universities. Unfortunately, the universities receive none of the **revenue**.

> *Q: What would happen to the market for entry-exam training if the Czech government allowed universities to charge higher tuition to noncitizens?*

Price Floors

4.9

My visiting eighty-three-year-old mother told the assembled family one of the oldest economics jokes under the sun. A lady went into a butcher shop and asked, "How much is the ground beef?" "It's $2.95 a pound," responded the butcher. "That's outrageous," said the lady. "The other butcher shop in town advertises it for $1.79 a pound." "Yes," said the butcher, "and I have it even cheaper than that when I also don't have it in stock." Telling customers that an item is priced very low when in fact none is in stock may be a good way of getting them into the store, but it will leave them unhappy because their **demand** exceeds the storekeeper's available supply.

*Q: Think about the market for labor instead of the market for ground beef. What does this joke tell you about the effect on the demand for low-skilled labor of proposals to set the **minimum wage** in the United States at $10 per hour?*

4.10

As a **price floor,** a minimum wage restricts the amount of goods, or inputs, that demanders are willing to buy. But what happens if the **demand curve** shifts to the left? If there were no floor, the price of the good or service would drop as the market moves down along the **supply curve,** and a new equilibrium price would be established. But with the floor, the price cannot drop—all that can happen is that the leftward shift in the demand curve must lead to a drop in the quantity employed. This is exactly what happens, according to a study of the labor market in Portugal. Among companies with a higher fraction of employees paid at the minimum wage, when demand for the product goes down, these companies are more likely to close down. The floor on wages imposed by the minimum prevents the companies from cutting costs, and the drop in product demand drives them out of business when they can no longer supply at a competitive price.

Q: This describes the response of companies that cannot afford to remain in business. What will happen to employment at those companies that stay in business?

4.11

A friend of mine attended a speech by the nation's leading advocate of a universal living wage. This idea is essentially a minimum wage on steroids: The minimum amount payable would be much higher than the current minimum wage; and some versions of the proposal mandate minimum benefits as well. The effects of this higher **price floor** on labor markets are in the same direction as those of a minimum wage: By reducing the amount of low-skilled labor demanded and creating a surplus of low-skilled workers at the required higher wage, it will reduce employment of low-skilled workers. The only difference between the universal living wage and the current minimum wage is that its negative effects will be bigger. Because the minimum is at a higher level, it will affect the market for many more workers.

> *Q: I think we need a living wage for professors—no professor should be paid less than $100,000 per year at any college or university in the country! Currently, only a very few schools even pay that much on average. What would be the effect at your school if my wishes were legislated nationwide?*

4.12

During much of the semester, my four weekly office hours are nearly empty. The students who show up then get a lot of individualized attention: There is a **surplus** in the market for my office hours. In the week before each midterm, office hours are jammed, with long lines of students seeking help and being urged to finish quickly: There is a **shortage** of office hours. What can be done to solve the peak-load problem, in which the supply is fixed but the demand varies greatly over the semester? Unless I spent thirty office hours in each midterm week, I would be unable to satisfy all the students. The best solution is advertising to shift demand from peak to slack times. Early in the semester, the students are told about this problem. The clever ones shift their visits to the previously slack times and hope to benefit more from their time in my office. It helps, but there is still a shortage right before exams and a surplus most of the time.

> *Q: Economists believe in using prices to eliminate disequilibriums in markets. If the professor could charge the students for office-hour visits, do you have any suggestions on how prices might be used to remove or at least reduce this problem? Are there any other nonmonetary incentives that the professor might use?*

4.13

In the movie *Stealing Harvard*, one main character goes into a convenience store and buys four six-packs of beer. He then walks out to a car where two teenagers have been waiting, and sells a six-pack to these underage kids for $20. His friend hears about this and is outraged that he would charge so much for a six-pack. He justifies his actions saying, "One way or another they were going to get drunk. They might have to drink mouthwash," so he views himself as increasing economic well-being by selling them the beer that they otherwise couldn't buy. In some sense, he is. The government has imposed a ban on drinking by minors, essentially the equivalent of a **price floor** of infinity. By supplying the beer at $20, he is helping society remove the rigidity of that price floor and getting consumers (the teenagers, in this case) the product at a price they are willing to pay.

> *Q: Instead of outlawing sales of beer to minors and implicitly setting a price of infinity, why doesn't the government just put a special high tax on liquor sales to minors? That way, those minors who wish to consume alcohol could do so, although at a high price.*

Quantity Restrictions

4.14

One of the favorite souvenirs in my office is a set of my grandpa's leftover gasoline *ration coupons* from World War II. These coupons, without which U.S. drivers could not buy gasoline during the war years, accompanied money in the purchase of this product: You needed a coupon and, for example, a quarter to buy a gallon of gasoline. By issuing coupons, the federal government both guaranteed that civilians had access to a fixed **supply** of gasoline and ensured that civilians in war-essential jobs had the opportunity to buy more than other civilians could. The system did not work badly, so my parents tell me, but would it work as well today? Actually, if the coupons could be traded, it probably would work better now. Markets, aided by computerized trading, would quickly spring up, and the coupons would very quickly wind up in the hands of those citizens who value them most at the margin rather than those who were fortunate enough to receive them. But if that were true, why give out the coupons in the first place? Why not just let the free market determine who gets the gasoline?

> *Q: What are the differences between what would happen in a free market and what would happen if tradable coupons had to be used?*

4.15

Cockfighting is outlawed in many states. Other states have recently passed laws outlawing it, and Congress has passed an act outlawing shipping fighting birds in interstate commerce. Cockfighting is a big industry—there's clearly a large demand for the product. The new laws restricting interstate shipments of fighting cocks will *reduce the supply* of birds, as fewer people will want to risk arrest and jail or fines under the new, wider laws. This will raise the price of this essential input into cockfighting. With this higher input price, the number of people willing to put on cockfights for customers will diminish. There will be less cockfighting—onlookers will be charged higher prices for the fights that remain.

> *Q:*   *Who loses out as a result of this federal intervention in the cockfighting market?*

4.16

At lunch today, someone mentioned a large "gentleman's club" (in Texas that means a topless bar) that is near a shopping center here and pointed out how successful it is. Someone else expressed surprise that Austin has so few bars with a naked wait staff. There's a very simple reason: State law allows selling alcohol by the drink in topless bars but not in other bars, and it is the sale of alcohol that generates profits for the bars. Bottomless clubs might well be preferred by many customers, but because they are not profitable under the restrictions imposed by state law, what customers probably view as an inferior **substitute** is much more widespread.

> *Q:*   *What would happen in the market for such venues if the state repealed the law allowing liquor sales only in topless bars? What would happen if the state passed a law outlawing tobacco use in all of these bars?*

CHAPTER 5

The Consumer—Elasticities and Incentives

Elasticity of Demand

5.1

I often do a survey of my students to see if their demand for places at the university responds to prices. The price of places at the university is the tuition charged. I offer students the possibility of zero tuition increase for next year, a 5 percent increase for next year, and a 10 percent increase. Each student is then asked whether he or she will return next year. I recently got the following results: For a 5 percent tuition increase, the number of students returning would decrease by 2.2 percent, implying a **price elasticity of demand** equaling −.44. For a 10 percent tuition increase, however, the number returning would fall by 11.8 percent, implying an elasticity of −1.18. The **demand curve** is surely downward sloping. Not only does the number of places demanded decline when tuition rises more; the responsiveness of demand—the price elasticity of demand—is greater in percentage terms when the university tries to raise tuition by higher amounts. That's not surprising: **Substitutes** that suddenly become slightly cheaper don't affect behavior proportionately as much as substitutes that suddenly become relatively a lot cheaper.

> *Q: Ask yourself the same question. List tuition increases for your school for next year, and ask how many of you and your friends are planning to return. Are your freshman friends more or less likely to return than your friends who are juniors?*

5.2

Today's *Wall Street Journal* carries a story that talks about airlines cutting business fares (fares on first-class seats) and finding their revenue doesn't drop. It says that Delta has cut fares by about 21 percent in small markets, without any special advertisements; it has experienced a "double-digit" increase in revenue. Assuming nothing else changed, this must mean that in those markets the demand for first-class tickets has a price elasticity of more than 1—the demand is **elastic**. Indeed, the "double-digit" increase (at least 10 percent), coupled with the 21 percent price decrease, implies that the **price elasticity of demand** is at least 1.5 ([10 + 21]/21).

   Q: What would have happened to revenue if the demand curve had been inelastic?

5.3

During class, a number of students were amused when they thought I had made an obscene gesture while pointing to something on the overhead. I hadn't, but it reminded me of a story. In spring 2000, I was taking a taxi from a conference center in rural Bavaria, Germany, to the Munich airport. Another driver did something really stupid, and I told the taxi driver that, in the United States, I would have given that an obscene gesture. He said he would, too, but there's a fine of 500 Deutschmarks (about $240) in Bavaria if one is caught doing that. I asked if there were other fines, and he mentioned a fine of 300 Deutschmarks for giving a certain other obscene gesture. The questions are: (1) Do these fines reduce the number of gestures given (do people move up the **demand curve** as the price rises)? (2) To what extent are different gestures **substitutes** whose consumption depends on the relative prices (the fines)? (3) More generally, what is the **price elasticity of demand** for giving obscene gestures?

   Q: How elastic do you think your own behavior would be in response to a difference in fines for different gestures? If the chance that you might be caught increases, what happens to your price elasticity of demand for giving obscene gestures?

5.4

An advertisement for a marketing consulting firm that offers seminars to businesses stated, "After you attend our seminars, your competitors will say that people would be fools to buy from anyone else, regardless of what prices you charge them." It is very hard to believe that all those **demand curves** are perfectly inelastic!

> *Q: If you believe this advertisement and run a business, what price will you charge your customers? Find another advertisement in today's newspaper, in a news magazine, or on television where a similarly ridiculous claim about the shape of the demand curve is implied.*

5.5

The local airport in Austin, Texas, opened in 1999 with on-site parking, priced from $18 per day for garage parking to $6 per day for distant uncovered parking. No other choices were offered and, despite the prices, the lots were so crowded that soon the Airport Authority built an additional lot. By 2002, off-site parking places had opened up, offering covered parking for $8 per day, and some offering three-minute shuttle service to the terminal (much faster than the on-site distant uncovered parking). Not surprisingly, this entry of new competitors into the parking market has left many on-site places empty, and the airport's parking revenues this year have fallen from $22 million to $18 million. If the Airport Authority is smart, it would think about what its demand elasticity is, lower prices if it believes demand is **elastic,** not lower them, and maybe even raise them (especially on garage parking) if it believes demand is **inelastic.** The evidence suggests management believes that the demand is elastic for the garage parking, because in 2004 they lowered the price for garage parking to $15 per day.

> *Q: For which part of the airport parking areas is the demand likely to be more or less elastic, the garage parking or the uncovered distant parking? In light of your beliefs about this question, how would you alter prices?*

5.6

Problem at the Coffee Shop. My favorite local coffee shop, located three doors down a side street near an intersection with a major road, faces its most severe challenge: Starbucks has set up shop on the corner. My shop sells better-tasting coffee than Starbucks, and it charges a lower price. Nonetheless, I fear it will be driven out of business. Having observed the shop's clientele for years, I have noticed that most are regulars. I have become friendly with the owner, and I suggest to him that he should raise his price. He will still be offering his coffee at a lower price than Starbucks. My guess is that his clients have a fairly **inelastic demand,** since they come both for the quality of the product and for the ambience. Also, they are in the habit of coming. Raising prices is unlikely to drive away many customers, and it will raise **revenue** and help the shop stay in business.

> *Q: If there is lots of mobility in the neighborhood—many old residents move out, and many new ones move in—what happens to the **price elasticity of demand** facing the shop owner?*

5.7

My mother-in-law telephoned my wife long distance, Boston to Austin, at least once and occasionally as many as three times a day, often at inconvenient times. She moved to Austin and lived there for the last six months of her life. In Boston, the calls cost her seven cents a minute. In Austin, they were local calls, with no extra charge assessed no matter how often she called. With a price per extra call equaling zero, did she call us even more than before? What was her **price elasticity of demand** for these calls? In fact, my wife was not deluged with calls. This may have been because my mother-in-law's **demand curve** shifted leftward. With her being in Austin, just two miles away from our house, my wife and I were able to visit her much more frequently than before. Perhaps personal visits and phone calls are **substitutes.** Alternatively, maybe the absence of many extra phone calls was due to her demand for phone calls being quite inelastic.

> *Q: Is your demand for long-distance calls fairly* price-inelastic *or* price-elastic? *If you own a cell phone, how has that affected your price elasticity of demand?*

5.8

An excellent example of product demand is for auto vanity license plates. Noneconomists might imagine that there's no economic decision making in choosing whether to buy a vanity plate—vanity is vanity, and why should price matter? But the plates seem to be a completely standard good. One study estimated a **price elasticity of demand** of −1.30 and an **income elasticity of demand** of +.57. What was especially neat about the results is that demand is higher if the state government spends more tax revenue promoting the sale of vanity plates and if the program has existed longer. Quality seems to matter, too: The more characters allowed on a vanity plate, the greater the sales.

> *Q: As with every good, the price elasticity of demand need not be constant across income classes. Do you think the demand is more or less elastic among higher-income families?*

5.9

Last summer saw record-breaking heat in southern France. The summer left the soil so parched that this winter's crop of French truffles, a fungus that is a gourmet favorite, is very small. This sharp *decrease in supply* has driven the price up to $1,250 per kilogram. Chinese truffles, which are a different species and do taste different (and, so French truffle gurus claim, are somewhat bitter and rubbery), are priced at "only" $25 per kilogram. Not surprisingly, some restaurateurs are substituting the cheaper Chinese truffles for their now much more expensive French cousins. French truffle-diggers have discovered that the demand for their produce is not quite as **inelastic** as they had believed. To reduce the elasticity of demand for their product, they are orchestrating campaigns to ban the description of the Chinese variety by the term "truffles."

> *Q: Why do the French truffle growers want to reduce the elasticity of demand for French truffles?*

Income Elasticity

5.10

The easiest example to use to understand elasticity is the behavior of the Cookie Monster on *Sesame Street*. As nearly every American under the age of thirty-five knows, the Cookie Monster (CM) eats only cookies. Assume that his income is $100 per week and that the price of a cookie is $1. If the price doubles, he cuts his consumption in half; the amount that he spends on cookies stays constant at $100. This means that CM's **price elasticity of demand** for cookies is exactly −1. His demand is **unit-elastic.** If the price is $1 and his weekly income doubles to $200, he doubles the number of cookies he buys. That means that CM's **income elasticity of**

demand for cookies is +1. For him, cookies are neither a **luxury** nor a **necessity,** but are on the very thin border in between.

*Q: Are pretzels **substitutes** or **complements** for cookies to the Cookie Monster?*

5.11

A young woman gets pregnant and decides to abort rather than bear the child. You would think that this is a highly personal decision in which economics couldn't play a role. Even in something as personal as this, though, prices and incomes seem to matter. A study of changes in interstate differences in abortions shows that where and when the price of an abortion is higher, the number of abortions is lower. The **price elasticity of demand** is around −1: The demand for abortions is essentially **unit-elastic.** At the same price, abortions are more common in those states and those times where incomes are higher: The **income elasticity of demand** for abortions is around +.5. Abortion is a **superior good,** but it is a **necessity,** not a **luxury.**

Q: Take another delicate procedure: liver transplants. Would you think the demand for liver transplants is more or less price-elastic than the demand for abortions? Explain your reasoning.

5.12

At my wife's office Christmas party, she "won" a set of bookplates, adhesive-backed paper that says "Ex Libris [from the library]" and on which you print your name below. These can be put on the inside covers of books you own. They are quite uncommon now but were very common until the 1960s. Why are they increasingly rare? They presumably indicate your ownership of something that others might borrow. Today, however, there is much less book borrowing than there used to be. First, with higher incomes, people buy books rather than borrow them. Books are *not* **inferior goods.** Second, paperbacks are now everywhere, and they were quite uncommon until the 1930s or 1940s. With the growth of the paperback market, there is much less interest in borrowing someone else's hardback copy.

Q: For the same tastes—same age and education—do people with higher incomes buy more or fewer books? If more, are books a **necessity** *or a* **luxury?***

5.13

The latest business-book fad is *Trading Up,* a tome by two retailing executives pointing out that consumers are buying more high-quality products than before. This trend should not surprise economics students: As people's incomes rise (and they have risen), in addition to buying more goods they will buy better-quality, more luxurious goods. Our theory of the consumer has her buying more as her income rises; but nobody needs more than one toaster, more than one washing machine, or more than one clothes dryer, to pick just a few products. Instead, consumers buy higher-quality goods—toaster-ovens, front-loading washing machines, humidity-sensitive clothes dryers, and so on. In looking at **income elasticities,** we need to remember that part of the impact of rising income is on the quality of goods purchased.

> *Q: What does this vignette suggest to you about how higher incomes might affect the variety of things that people buy or do, as well as their quantity?*

5.14

Between 1990 and 2000, the rate of workplace injuries in the United States fell 25 percent. Workplace fatalities fell even more. These changes accelerated a trend toward safer workplaces that had been observed for many years. Are these changes the result of increased government concern about worker safety? Maybe, but the trend is also consistent with the fact that safety in the workplace is a **superior good:** As people's incomes rise, they are willing to forgo some extra earnings in order to obtain more safety on the job. Whether job safety is a **luxury** or a **necessity** is not clear, but it is certainly not an **inferior good:** The **income elasticity of demand** for safety is positive.

> *Q: What does this vignette suggest has happened to the rate of deaths from auto accidents since 1950? Check on the Web to see whether your inference is correct.*

5.15

Seattle residents recently voted on whether to impose a 10 cent tax on espresso drinks, the so-called "latte tax." What would be the effects of this tax by income category? It depends on who drinks lattes, but I would guess that the demand for latte is income elastic—latte is a **luxury good.** That being the case, the latte tax would fall disproportionately on higher-income consumers and would thus tend to reduce inequality. The only question is whether the tax might generate a large decrease in latte consumption—how price elastic is the demand for lattes? I would think the demand is fairly **inelastic,** so that latte buyers would not decrease the quantity demanded very much as prices rise in response to the imposition of the tax. Seattle voters, in fact, rejected the tax, thus implicitly refusing to create a tax that would make after-tax incomes more equal.

Q: What if a tax had instead been proposed on regular coffee rather than espresso drinks? What would its burden be on people of different income categories?

Incentives

5.16

On its Web site, the university makes available the distribution of the course grades each professor gives out. One of my clever young colleagues knows this and says that he likes to give out a lot of As and a lot of Fs. This gives the students whom he wants to take his course an incentive to do so while discouraging the students he doesn't want. Students who might normally be B students think they can get an A and sign up. Students who are C or D students believe that they have a much higher than usual chance of getting an F and stay away from his courses. His grade distribution thus allows students voluntarily to sort themselves in a way that maximizes the quality of the students taking his class.

Q: Ask yourself and your friends: Would you respond to this information the way my colleague believes students do?

5.17

Last year the Texas legislature passed a law allowing auto insurers to set prices on the basis of the mileage actually driven. This seems like a good idea. Hamburgers are priced on a per-unit basis; why not price compensation for the risk of accident the same way? If that were done, people who drive relatively little would no longer be **subsidizing** the ones who drive 50,000 miles a year.

Unfortunately, no insurer has yet chosen to offer this kind of pricing. I'm not surprised: How can insurers determine the mileage actually driven by each particular insured driver? Unless everyone is completely honest, cheating drivers will guarantee that insurers will lose money on this basis. The end result will be no insurance offered—or a return to the pricing scheme we now have.

Q: How would the outcome in this market differ if the insurance companies could monitor your driving electronically? Would that solve all the problems?

5.18

One of the textbooks I assign will have a new edition this July 2005 with a copyright date of 2006. It used to be that a book used the next year's copyright date only if it appeared after September 1 of the current year. That restriction seems to have broken down. So why not publish the book in January 2005 with a 2006 copyright? That way people will think it is current long after it comes out, and it might sell for longer. In textbook publishing, the answer is clear: The publishers don't want the books to last too long because the used-book market eats away at sales. Getting a small advantage by labeling a book published in July 2005 as copyrighted in 2006 gives an extra profit. Any further "jumping the gun" confers no great advantage. In other areas, however, such as college football bowl bids and job offers, there are big incentives for people to start making deals ahead of previously agreed deadlines. Eventually, some of those deadlines break down as a few buyers and sellers realize that it is to their advantage to agree on a deal ahead of the deadline. This breakdown has happened several times in college football bowl bids, although colleges now adhere closely to the deadlines of the Bowl Championship Series (BCS).

Q: If you are the manager of the Fruit Bowl, a new bowl game, and have lots of money to bid for bowl participants, would you wait for the BCS picks to be determined? How early would you begin offering bowl berths?

5.19

One of the perks of being a faculty member is paid travel for professional activities, usually to appear on the program at a scholarly meeting or convention. In my first year as department chair, I was deluged with requests by my colleagues that the university fund such travel. It was very hard for me to say no and, at the end of the year, I noticed that spending for faculty travel was more than twice what had been budgeted. One colleague had taken seven paid trips during the year. I didn't know what to do: I didn't want to spend my time deciding which proposed trips were meritorious and which were not, and I didn't want to have to say no to my colleagues. One new faculty member solved the problem. He said, "Just tell each faculty member: You have a certain amount—a lump sum [it turned out to be $750]— for professional travel. Spend it any way you want, so long as it is a justifiable professional trip." This solved the problem completely: no more complaining and no more budget overruns. Each professor knew what his or her budget was when the year started and was able to choose the best possible trip or combination of trips. The young colleague had reminded me that it's always better to have a lump sum to spend than to be required to spend the same sum on a specified set of activities that you can't choose freely.

> *Q: Think back to when you lived at home. Is my problem in this vignette in any way different from your parents' choice of whether to give you a fixed weekly allowance or to spend the same amount of money on specific things for you?*

5.20

The dean of our liberal arts college wants to get more of the 500 faculty members to submit proposals to foundations and governments to obtain funding for their research. If you submit a proposal, he would give you a grant of $2,000 to be used for academic travel, book purchases, computers, and the like. This incentive is designed to get faculty members to do things they otherwise would not do; it raises the returns to submitting a grant proposal. The dean's idea has two problems. The obvious one is how to police the proposals: What's to prevent me from submitting a slipshod proposal that has no chance of outside funding so that I can get the dean's $2,000? The bigger problem—one that is inherent in any **subsidy**—is how can he avoid subsidizing proposals that would have been written anyway? How can he subsidize only the marginal proposals and avoid giving the $2,000 grants to faculty members who already had planned to seek funding? He can't; his only hope is that the **elasticity of supply** of proposals is sufficiently high that many faculty members who had been just below the margin where they would apply for grants are induced to write proposals.

*Q: Draw a **supply curve** of proposals where the dean's subsidy will create a lot of new proposals. Draw one where his subsidy will not have much effect.*

5.21

July 2003—The children's movie *Spy Kids 3* premieres tomorrow—in Austin, Texas! The local newspaper reports that tickets are being offered under a pricing scheme that charges $1,000 for an individual adult or $750 for an adult accompanied by a child. This gives every adult who wants to see the movie an incentive to find a kid to bring along. The moviemaker presumably cooked up this pricing scheme because he wants to make sure that a large part of the audience is children. And he's likely to succeed: Unless you hate kids so much that you are willing to pay $250 to avoid being in charge of a child for two hours, you will find a kid to take with you. This pricing scheme creates incentives for the consumer that will achieve the producer's desires.

Q: What would happen to the mix of the audience if the price for an unaccompanied adult were $900 instead of $1,000? What about if the price for an adult with a kid were only $500?

5.22

What cell phone plan to get? The issue is the unrestricted minutes, usable at any time. They are offered on a two-part price system: You pay a fixed amount for a maximum number of minutes and then pay per minute for any time above that. The price of an extra minute is zero up to the limit; thereafter, it becomes quite high. (One company offers 250 anytime minutes for a fixed fee of $30, offers 350 minutes for a fixed fee of $40, and charges 35 cents a minute if you exceed your limit.) Having bought a particular plan, you have a tremendous incentive to use all your minutes. You also have an incentive to be very careful as you near the maximum, since the cost of exceeding it is high. If you're repeatedly using more than your maximum, you have bought a plan that doesn't have enough minutes: You can do better with more guaranteed minutes. Indeed, you should buy a plan that you are nearly certain you will never exceed. That way there is no need to incur the **opportunity cost** of monitoring how many minutes remain.

> *Q: This kind of pricing scheme seems unusual. What would the incentives be if the cell phone companies simply priced on a per-minute basis, with no fixed charge but a higher price for anytime minutes than for weekend minutes? Would you spend more or less on your cell-phone service?*

5.23

We toured St. Basil's, the Orthodox cathedral near Red Square, Moscow, which is probably the most familiar sight in Russia. On the wall in one of the chapels was a description stating that Czar Ivan the Terrible, who had commissioned building it, thought the cathedral was so beautiful that he had the architect blinded so that he could never again create something as beautiful. Ivan was clearly not a nice guy—but he also wasn't a very good economist. The next time he needed a builder, the (remaining sighted) architects had tremendous incentives to do good, but not great jobs, lest they too be blinded. By blinding the architect, Ivan ensured that he, too, would never get another building as magnificent as St. Basil's.

> *Q: How would Ivan's incentives to put out the eyes of architects differ early versus late in his reign?*

5.24

A senior who was scheduled to graduate this term was failing a course. He decided to download a term paper and turn it in as his own work. Since his prior record was clean, the university's most severe punishment for cheating in this case is for him to fail the course. The student clearly optimized in light of the **incentives** he faced. Had he cheated and not been caught, he would have passed the course and graduated. Had he not cheated, his complete lack of knowledge of the course's material meant that he would surely have failed and not graduated. Cheating and getting caught leave him no worse off than he would have been if he hadn't cheated at all (ignoring any moral qualms he should have had), and he at least had a chance of getting away with it and graduating.

Q: What could the university do to alter the incentives facing graduating seniors to make the less moral ones behave better?

5.25

A story on National Public Radio this morning talked about the effects of differences among American states in whether health insurers must pay for in vitro fertilization. In states where coverage is mandatory, fewer fertilized eggs are implanted per try than in states where the procedure is not covered. The reason is simple: If a woman wants to get pregnant, she has a greater chance of a successful pregnancy the more fertilized ova that are implanted. And, since each implantation costs her money directly if she is not covered, she has an incentive to minimize the number of separate procedures. Creating this incentive minimizes insurers' costs in the short run, and it also reduces costs in the long run. With fewer eggs implanted at one time, there's a smaller chance of multiple births. Since multiple births are much more costly than single births and, since health insurers usually cover the cost of births, the incentives they have created for in vitro fertilization also reduce the number of expensive multiple births.

Q: What if health insurers covered LASIK eye surgery, the surgical reduction of nearsightedness? How would that affect incentives, and what would that do to the market for eyeglasses? How would the effects differ by age of the population?

CHAPTER 6

*T*he Consumer— How to Choose

Utility

6.1

Utility is funny. I lived perfectly well for years without a cell phone and without a cable modem (using land phones and a dial-up connection), and right after I got them, I did not feel all that much happier. At this point, though, if they were taken away, I'd feel much worse. There's an asymmetry or ratcheting effect on happiness, at least in the short run, which keeps raising our so-called needs for goods once we have gotten used to them. Our utility depends not only on what we are currently consuming, but also on what we are accustomed to consuming.

> *Q: What new goods that you have can't you live without? If one of them were taken away, would you feel worse? Would you continue to feel worse for years, or would your negative feelings diminish?*

6.2

Suicide is an extremely depressing topic, but one can think about it like an economist. One can imagine people rationally choosing to kill themselves if they expect little **utility** over the remainder of their natural lives. Since life expectancies are lower the older you are, an economist would expect higher suicide rates among older people, and that's exactly what we see happening. Similarly, unemployment also lowers people's satisfaction, and we know that suicide rates rise in recessions. Someone who experiences a sudden drop in income is also more likely to commit suicide. Economic factors aren't the only cause of suicide—far from it—but they do matter, and we can use simple economics to be on the lookout for people who might be contemplating suicide.

Q: Can you use the same arguments to predict who is more likely to commit murder? Why or why not?

6.3

Several years ago, an economist asked undergraduates to place values on gifts received from various people. Gifts from girl-friends or boyfriends were valued at almost $1 per $1 price of the gift, and presents from parents at somewhat less. Relative to the students' valuations, presents from grandparents had the least value per $1 the grandparents actually spent on the presents. It's possible that the source of the gift matters: A present from a girl-friend or boyfriend is valued more than the identical present from one's grandparents. An economist would say, though, that girlfriends and boyfriends know your **utility** function best, while grandparents are almost clueless about what does or does not make you happier.

Q: If you had been one of the student participants in the study discussed here, how would you value a typical present costing $100 from your parents, your Aunt Sadie, your boyfriend or girl-friend, your grandmother?

6.4

I just received the $2,000 referred to in a vignette in Chapter 5. The problem is that these funds must be spent on academic travel, book purchases, computers, and so forth. Worse still, they must be spent by August 31. The funds come with both a goods constraint and a time constraint. My **utility** would be higher if I could just take the funds as a nontaxable monetary gift. That way, I could spend them over an extended period on exactly the goods and ser-vices that maximize my utility. This is always true: We can always be at least as well off with unrestricted money as with money whose use is restricted (since, without the restrictions, we could always buy the things to which the restrictions limit us). We are also at least as well off with money whose spending has no dead-line as with money that must be spent soon. What should I do?

I could just use up the money on things that are not too valuable to me. Better still, though, I should find a legitimate way to break the restrictions that prevent my using the money after August 31.

> *Q: Imagine yourself getting $1,000 from your rich uncle that has to be spent on clothing in the next week. What would you buy? How would you circumvent the restrictions the rich uncle imposes?*

6.5

My wife insisted on giving me a big birthday treat for my sixtieth birthday. The prices were outrageous, though: $450 for a good ticket to the Rolling Stones concert, or $250 for a good ticket to Cirque du Soleil's "O." What to do? For the Stones' concert to be worthwhile, it must yield me 9/5 ($450/$250) as much satisfaction as "O" when I compare the relative marginal utilities of each to the ratio of their prices. In this case, the choice was easy: We bought the Stones' tickets and attended the most memorable concert of my life.

> *Q: Can we tell from my decision how low the price of "O" tickets would have to have been to lead me to choose to go to see "O"? Why or why not?*

6.6

Today is a great day in economic research. A study of mine, written jointly with a former colleague, has been accepted for publication in a leading scholarly journal. Both he and I are very happy about it. For a professor, getting recognition for your ideas is always very gratifying and, in my profession, publication outlets form a clear hierarchy, with this one near the top. This outlet had previously published thirteen papers by my ex-colleague, but none of mine. The **marginal utility** of the fourteenth paper published in that journal must be less than the marginal utility of the first. If we are both rational and have the same preferences, then I should be much happier about having this study accepted for publication than he is.

> *Q: I have had many scholarly papers published over my thirty-eight-year career in economics, many of them in others of the very top scholarly journals in the field. What's special about this one?*

66   ECONOMICS IS EVERYWHERE

6.7

I was lucky enough to read to four grandkids the story "Murmel, Murmel, Murmel," in *Munschworks 2* by kids' author Robert Munsch. In the story, five-year-old Robin finds a baby in a hole in a sandbox. She begins looking for someone to care for the child. She asks a woman, who answers, "Heavens no, I already have a baby." She asks an old lady, who says, "I already have seventeen cats [presumably babies and cats are **substitutes**]." She then asks another woman, who responds, "Heavens no, I have seventeen jobs, lots of money, and no time [illustrating the **opportunity cost** of having kids]." She asks a man, who, when told the baby will not wash his car and can't be sold for lots of money [babies today are mostly consumption items, not used for production], also says no. She finally asks a truck driver, who sees the baby, happily takes it, and walks off, leaving his truck. Robin says, "Wait, you forgot your truck." He says, "I already have seventeen trucks. What I need is a baby." The **marginal utility** of the seventeenth truck was very low for him; the marginal utility of the first baby was very high.

> *Q: What is something you have lots of and that costs the same as something you don't have? Why don't you switch?*

6.8

One of the students grasped the notion of equating the **marginal utility** per dollar of expenditure on different items in a very concrete and personal manner. He noted that he received a $100 gift certificate for Best Buy recently. The choice as he saw it was to spend the money on DVDs at a price of $25 each, or on video games at $50 each. He realized that if he spent the $100 on video games, each one had to yield a marginal utility twice that of DVDs to justify its purchase. Otherwise, he could increase his utility more by spending the gift certificate on DVDs, since his extra utility per dollar of extra spending would then be greater.

> *Q: How would the student's choices differ is DVDs and video games cost the same? How about if DVDs cost only $10 each?*

6.9

The Big Texan Steak Ranch and Opry in Amarillo, Texas, offers the following deal: "Eat The Big Texan's famous 72 oz. steak dinner with all the trimmings (appetizer, salad, and potato) in one hour and it's FREE! Almost 35,000 people have tried and 5,500 have succeeded." But you must eat it all—you can't eat part and throw the rest away. Let's say you really only want to eat a small amount, say only sixty-four ounces, and that eating the remaining eight ounces makes you worse off (feelings of bloat and even nausea). The marginal utility of the last eight ounces is actually negative. It might still be sensible to eat the whole thing if the loss in utility from eating the last eight ounces is smaller than the gain in utility that results when you save the cost of buying the steak dinner because you ate it all. With this unusual pricing scheme, it could pay to keep on consuming, even though the **marginal utility** is less than zero, if that is the only way you can get the pleasure of the first sixty-four ounces.

Q: Give two examples of "all-or-nothing" deals that you have seen. Have you bought them? Why or why not?

6.10

At a restaurant last night, the menu had an eight-ounce filet mignon for $21 and a twelve-ounce filet mignon for $26. I ordered the eight-ounce filet, while a colleague ordered the twelve-ounce version. I expressed surprise and doubt that he would really want to eat that much meat. He responded, "I am not sure that I want to eat the extra four ounces, but at least I now have the option of doing so, and at the very low marginal price of $5 to get 50 percent more steak." If an extra bit of something is cheap enough, even if we think its **marginal utility** is very low, it is rational to purchase it just for the option of having it available to consume in the future.

Q: Assume you would have done the same thing as my colleague. Would you still do it if the price of the twelve-ounce filet had been $28? If you would not have mimicked my colleague when the price was $26, how low would the price of the twelve-ounce steak have to drop before you bought it instead of the eight-ounce steak for $21?

6.11

Texas and some other states are dotted with sheds selling fireworks on a seasonal basis (before New Year's Day and before July 4). Many of them offer, "Buy one, get five free." Why don't they just cut the price from, for example, $6 per item to $1 per item and sell them one at a time? Would their **revenue** be the same if they did? I assume not, or they would do that. There are several reasons why their behavior might make sense. First and most important, this gimmick lowers the price of each of the second through sixth firecrackers to zero. Since the cost of each extra firecracker is zero, you will be willing to spend more in total than you would if each were priced at the same positive amount. If the fireworks seller is clever, the total cost of the six exactly equals the sum of what you would have been willing to pay for the first plus for the second plus for the third, and so on. This is similar to pricing of ski lifts, "all you can eat" buffets, and other such deals. In all these cases, the seller is hoping, by charging the equivalent of a fixed fee for purchasing the goods or services, to get the buyer to spend more. In economists' jargon, the seller is hoping to extract the entire **consumer surplus** from the buyers, to obtain revenue equal to the entire area under each buyer's **demand curve** for the product.

Q: What might lead a seller to offer "Buy one, get five free," as opposed to offering "Buy one, get ten free"?

6.12

My eight-year-old grandson has a difficult problem. His parents are now limiting him to one hour a day on electronic media—his Gameboy, television viewing, and Web surfing. Also, he cannot spend more than 30 minutes on any one of these. The opportunity cost of a minute of time on each is the same—it's one minute of time spent on one of the other two. Without these restrictions, he would no doubt consume each so that the **marginal utility** of the last minute on each of the three is identical. But his parents' restrictions may make that impossible. Indeed, knowing him, I would think that he spends 30 minutes on the Gameboy. Even then, its marginal utility exceeds that of the first minute on the TV or the Web. He probably then takes the remaining 30 minutes and allocates it the usual way between the two other activities, devoting time to each so that the marginal utility of the last minute on the Web and on watching television is the same.

Q: Would my grandson be happier or less happy if his parents also said he has to spend at least ten minutes on each one of the three activities? Would he be happier or less happy if he could spend as much or as little of the hour on each activity as he wants?

6.13

At Reliant Stadium in Houston, Texas, you can buy beer while you watch football; but on Sundays the law prevents you from buying beer before noon unless you buy food along with it. What to do if the game starts at noon and you arrive at 11:30 AM and are thirsty? The stadium management solves your problem: For only $4, you can buy a bag of peanuts along with your $5 beer. Since peanuts count as food under the law, you are not doing anything illegal. Now $4 is an outrageous price for a few peanuts; but it is still less than the **consumer surplus** you get from buying the $5 beer when you're thirsty, so customers willingly, although probably not happily, shell out $5 for the beer and $4 more for the peanuts in order to buy the beer legally.

Q: If a customer buys the beer-and-peanuts combination before noon on a Sunday and throws away the peanuts, what do we know about the size of the consumer surplus that he obtains from a $5 beer?

6.14

I am sitting at a pizza joint with my son and his family. The eight-year-old grandson notices that on the children's menu there are unlimited "free refills" for soft drinks, but only one "free refill" for juice (orange juice, apple juice, etc.). He asks his mother and me why. He believes that it is because moms want their kids to drink juice and are willing to pay for lots of refills, whereas they won't pay for lots of soft drinks. This is a very good argument, and it may be correct. Another way of looking at my grandson's argument is that the pizza place can extract more **consumer surplus** by charging what is essentially a fixed price for as many soft drinks as you will swallow, but extracts more by charging for juices on a per-item basis. It might be that the demands are sufficiently different, with the moms' demands for kids' juice being less elastic, as my grandson believes, to make this a clever profit-maximizing pricing policy.

   Q: If eight-year-olds were completely free to buy whatever drinks they want, what pricing policy would you use in a restaurant like this?

6.15

In the movie *Pretty Woman*, Richard Gere and Julia Roberts are bargaining over the price of her "services" for a week. They settle on a price of $3,000. She informs him that she would have stayed for $2,000; implicitly, she obtains a **producer surplus** of $1,000, the excess of what she receives over the lowest price for which she would have provided the services. Richard Gere then goes on to say that he would have paid her $4,000. He is getting $1,000 in **consumer surplus**—the price he has to pay is $1,000 less than the highest amount he was willing to pay.

   Q: What is the consumer surplus if Richard Gere had been willing to pay only $3,500? Would the movie have been made if he had been willing to pay only $2,500?

Voting, Addiction, Altruism, and Risk

6.16

My Ph.D. student is agonizing about which of several jobs to accept. He has two offers so far, School A and School B. He tells me that he unquestionably would prefer School A to School B, but he wants to wait to reject School B until he hears whether he will be getting an offer from School C, which is his top choice. Is he being rational? No! If he prefers A to B, having C as an extra choice should not affect that preference ranking. Economists and social theorists call this notion the **independence of irrelevant alternatives.** The student was very upset when I called him "irrational" (probably the worst thing you can say to an economist) and began trying to explain how his reasoning was sensible. In the end, though, he laughed and admitted that he wasn't being very rational. But he still refuses to say no to School B until he finds out about School C.

   Q: What if School C is preferred to School B, but not to School A? Would waiting on School C make more or less sense than it did in the vignette? Would it be rational?

6.17

San Francisco has enacted an "instant runoff" rule; henceforth, people will rank their preferences for candidates when they vote. If there are three candidates and none wins a majority, the top two candidates are assigned the second-place votes of those who voted for the third candidate. Will people's first-place votes be the same as they are in the usual U.S. voting method? They should be: The **independence of irrelevant alternatives** suggests that including a second-place vote should not affect your first-place vote. Even if people do exhibit this independence, the voting scheme can result in outcomes totally different from those of a system that allows the candidate with a plurality to win. In my class in fall 1992, the students voted for president by ranking Clinton, Bush, and Perot. The first-place votes were 38 percent, 28 percent, and 34 percent. That eliminated Bush, but even though Clinton had won a plurality, Perot received almost all the second-place votes. If the sentiment in my class had been national, and if we used preferential voting to aggregate individuals' tastes, we would have had President Perot from 1993 through 1997.

> *Q: In 1996 Perot was on the ballot again (with Clinton and Dole). President Clinton received only 49 percent of the vote. Would the "instant runoff" system have made a difference then? What does that tell you about the conditions when that system will give results different from those of our usual voting system?*

6.18

Marginal utility diminishes, but not always very rapidly. On our first day together, my four-year-old granddaughter has been going down the waterslide into the pool at the beach house we are renting, and she shows no signs of getting tired of it (even though my wife and I are very tired of watching her). She must have gone down thirty times in a row. Finally, and fortunately, she decides she is finished, suggesting that the marginal utility has diminished and some other activity (being read to) is now more appealing. My question is: Is going down the waterslide **addictive** for her? Will she do it more times tomorrow? The answer turns out to be no—she goes down the waterslide a lot each day, but her interest seems to diminish across the days. I infer that watersliding into a swimming pool is not addictive for a four-year-old.

> Q: Are there any things that you see little kids do that are
> addictive, where they do more and more on each separate day or
> week?

6.19

I'm nearing the end of writing this book. My wife says I won't be able to stop and accuses me of being addicted. How can I be addicted? Don't I have **diminishing marginal utility,** so that the extra pleasure from writing each additional vignette is lower than the pleasure from writing the previous one? How can people be addicted? Don't they, too, get less and less extra pleasure from each extra cigarette, each extra injection of heroin, and so on? It's true that marginal utility diminishes at each point in time: Writing the third vignette in one day is less pleasurable than writing the first, and smoking the sixtieth cigarette yields less extra pleasure than smoking the first. But the first vignette written after having accumulated **addiction** capital—having generated lots of experience writing them—may yield more satisfaction than writing the first vignette on the day this book was started. The first cigarette smoked each day after having accumulated the addiction capital from a lifetime of smoking may yield more smoking pleasure than did the first cigarette smoked when you just began smoking. Utility has to be considered in light of the habits that one has invested in over one's lifetime—or in this case, over the duration of writing this book.

> Q: List two things you do that meet the definition of addiction
> as implied in this vignette. Are they really addictions? Have
> you really gotten more pleasure out of the first one consumed
> in a day (or in a week) as you have consumed more over your
> lifetime?

6.20

It's our wedding anniversary, and I was thinking about the most important things we have produced: our sons (and indirectly our grandchildren). We have decided to promise them each a sum of money as a gift every year for the next eight years. We think about this as follows: The **marginal utility** to us of these extra dollars of our own consumption must be less than the marginal utility to us of the sons' families' marginal spending from this money. How far does this intergenerational **altruism** go, and why? We certainly wouldn't give anywhere near this kind of money to our nieces or nephews, even though one niece could use it a lot.

Q: Would we give as much money if our grandchildren were adopted? Would our behavior differ if we were seventy-three years old instead of fifty-eight years old? Would we give more or less?

6.21

Nearly every organized religion has a text conveying a sentiment like "Do unto others as you would have them do unto you." This is an **altruistic** sentiment—implying that an increase in another person's **utility** should raise your utility. Yet George Bernard Shaw wrote, "Do not do unto others as you would that they should do unto you. Their tastes may not be the same." The cynical Irish writer had a point: I may view my actions in "helping" somebody else as an altruistic act, but the person "helped" will be worse off if he or she dislikes the goods or services provided. There is only one guaranteed way to raise another person's utility, at least in the short run—give him or her money. That way you are not imposing your preferences, since the recipient can spend the money on anything he or she wants.

Q: What does this argument tell you about the desirability of giving dollars to charity, as opposed to donating used clothing and furniture?

6.22

Defibrillators (machines designed to restore heart rhythm during a heart attack) are dropping in price so rapidly that they will soon be affordable by individuals for home use. Some doctors applaud this development. Others are concerned that people, knowing that the defibrillators provide some protection, will reduce their efforts to stay healthy and engage in more risky behavior. Of course that's true: Whenever you are provided insurance, you take more risks. The question is, What will be the net effect? On this general issue there is a lot of guidance. For example, one study that examined the impact of sex education showed that it does increase the amount of teenage sexual activity, but does not affect the rate of teen pregnancy. A similar thing probably will happen with home defibrillators: People will take a little bit less care, but the net effect will be that heart attack deaths at home decline.

Q: Can you infer from this example what the likely effect of laws requiring the use of seat belts might be on driving speeds and deaths in automobile accidents?

6.23

The old saying "A bird in the hand is worth two in the bush" is a fairly profound statement about risk and people's attitudes toward risk. If people don't care about risk at all, the saying that the utility from one bird in the hand equals the utility from two birds in the bush must mean that the chance of catching a bird is .5 (50 percent), since the expected catch is one bird. But if people don't like risk (are **risk-averse**), the chance of catching a bird has to be higher than .5: The only way that one in the hand equals two in the bush, if you don't like risk, can be if the expected number of birds caught is more than one bird. We think that most people are risk-averse. The best evidence for this assumption is that risky investments must yield higher returns if they are to attract investors. This old proverb must be implying that the chance of catching a bird in the bush is greater than 50 percent. How much greater depends on how much you dislike risk, how risk-averse you are.

Q: Most of us do not catch birds. But there are other activities where we can get all or nothing or something in between, say, an A or a C in a course, as opposed to a B. Which would you rather have, a 50 percent chance at an A and a 50 percent chance at a C, or the certainty of getting a B?

6.24

In Genesis 31:41, after Laban pursues him, Jacob berates Laban, "I served thee fourteen years for thy two daughters, and six years for thy flock; and thou hast changed my wages ten times." Jacob is not merely complaining about the long time spent. He is also unhappy about the uncertainty arising from Laban's constantly altering the income Jacob would receive from working for him. Even for the same average level of income, most people do not like variations around that level—they are **risk-averse.** They are even willing to give up a little bit of return in order to avoid uncertainty. Jacob's complaint mirrors the same motive underlying investors' insistence on large expected returns if they are asked to undertake a risky investment—they must be compensated for uncertainty.

> *Q: What about your job choices—would you prefer a job paying $30,000 a year, or one that has a 50 percent chance of paying $40,000 and a 50 percent chance of paying $20,000?*

6.25

I had a long-planned spring break trip to Israel to spend four days doing research with a coauthor and two days touring with my wife. The benefits of this trip are obvious: a fun vacation and a chance to get some interesting research accomplished. The only monetary cost if I don't make the trip is the $150 cancellation fee on the air ticket. But the potential cost of going is much larger and was looming larger with each additional Palestinian suicide bombing. The potential cost includes the loss from death or injury in such an attack times the risk of my becoming a victim. The risk is tiny, but the value to me of my life is huge. Figure it this way: Assume that I value my life at $10 million, about what economic experts use in their calculations. As long as the extra risk of death while there compared to staying at home is greater than $10 million/$150, in other words one chance in 66,667, it pays to cancel the trip. I'm uncertain what the extra risk is, but my **risk aversion** and concerns expressed by many family members made us decide to cancel.

> *Q: How should my decision have been affected if I value my life at $1 million? At $20 million? How would you analyze the issue if I refused to place a value on my life?*

6.26

A large chain store is offering shoppers an unusual price break: If you make a large enough purchase, you can take a card from a deck. You then scratch off the covering, just as with a lottery scratch ticket, and uncover a picture showing that you have won a discount. Some cards show a 10 percent discount, some 20 percent, and some 30 percent. Why doesn't the store offer the same discount to everyone, say, 20 percent off? If people were always **risk-averse,** that would be a smart move. They aren't: A visit to the local racetrack or to Las Vegas demonstrates that. The store is offering shoppers an opportunity to gamble while they shop. Within a certain range of outcomes (most people wouldn't take bad gambles on their lives or with their life savings), people like the risks that gambling offers them. The store hopes to attract customers by taking advantage of that preference.

> *Q: Ask yourself: In this situation, would you prefer a store where you knew that half the cards had a 10 percent discount and half had a 30 percent discount, or one where a third of the cards had 10 percent, a third had 20 percent, and a third had 30 percent?*

6.27

Do students like risk or, like most other people, are they **risk-averse?** I'm not sure. Judging by the student who persisted in walking in the middle of the road on campus today, oblivious to the risk of death and injury from the cars trying to avoid him, they seem to like taking risks. Yet when they aren't daydreaming, students are probably as risk-averse as the average citizen. The best evidence comes during class registration. We list lots of sections of introductory economics, some with instructors' names shown and others without a name. The students say that, for the same class time, they will invariably pick the section with the instructor's name listed. This is true even if it is not one of our better teachers. The reason is that they'd rather have someone who is just "OK" than take a chance that they might be in a section with a dreadful teacher who is assigned to the "no-name" sections. They don't seem to want to gamble that the unlisted instructor might be very good.

> *Q: You face a choice between a section of a course with no instructor's name listed and another one of the same size, at the same time, but with an instructor who you believe is an average teacher. Which section would you register for?*

6.28

Today is Administrative-Professional Appreciation Day (formerly Secretaries' Day). Each of thirty-two staff people in a local office received a check for $25 from the management. Each name also was entered into a raffle to win one of eight $100 bills. People generally like lotteries; they'll gamble a small amount for a chance to win big, even though on average they lose money on the deal. For small gambles, they behave as if they loved risk. In this case, though, the office manager received loud complaints about the gamble, with one senior secretary saying, "I'd rather that each person received $50 [the same cost to the law firm]." Is the office staff unusual in that these people seemed to be **risk-averse** and to prefer safety to a gamble that cost them nothing and gave a few people a big return? Or is something else going on? Perhaps the staff's attitudes also involved feelings of envy and concerns about fairness; perhaps they didn't think it fair that a few might receive a lot while the rest received nothing.

Q: How do you think the staff's attitudes would differ if each staff member had been required to put up $25 for a one-fourth chance of winning $100?

Tips on Hunting for Economics Everywhere in Part 1

1. Look at your own behavior and your friends' and family's behavior when you buy things or undertake a new activity. How does scarcity lead to that behavior?
2. Consider what is given up when another thing is chosen. What is the true opportunity cost of the choice?
3. Look at the choices society makes when the government spends tax dollars. What is being obtained, and what is it worth? What is forgone when the choice is made?
4. Look for cases where the government or another outside force restricts the ability of prices to equilibrate a market. Look, too, at cases where governments limit the quantity available.
5. Look at how people change their behavior when the actual or implicit price of an activity or good changes. Are the responses large or small?
6. Consider how purchases change as income changes. How do these differences in purchases vary by demographic characteristics?
7. Look at your own behavior as it reflects the satisfaction you get from different activities. Is it rational in terms of your objectives? Does it reflect diminishing marginal utility and a balancing of marginal utilities and prices?
8. What does behavior imply about attitudes toward risk? What does it show about altruism or envy?

PART 2

*P*roduction, Cost, and Markets

CHAPTER 7

Production and Cost

Production and Technology

7.1

A group of sorority members was describing to me how they were searching for a new housemother. Housemothering is an extremely specialized occupation, one requiring people skills, some managerial ability, and the willingness by a typically older adult to reside in a house filled with college students. It is difficult to find such people and difficult for interested people to find jobs. Fortunately, the market is big enough to make it profitable for a company to specialize in matching jobseekers with sororities or fraternities that are trying to hire. This particular sorority has retained this company's services. In a smaller country, one might imagine that the efficiency in matching jobs with workers that the firm provides wouldn't exist. There would not be enough jobs each year to support a company that specializes in matching student groups with housemothers. Here is a case where the tremendous size of the U.S. market allows **economies of scale** to arise in the production of an unusual service.

> *Q: In a smaller market, what kinds of institutions might arise to match people seeking jobs like this with sororities and fraternities that are looking for housemothers? In what ways might these other institutions not be as efficient as a specialized company?*

7.2

One of the most important sources of scarcity in the United States is transplantable organs. About one-sixth of people needing kidney transplants die before a suitable organ is found; and the situation is much worse for liver and heart transplants. A story on the *CBS Evening News* described the plight of three recent transplant patients. Each had found a friend or relative to donate a kidney, but none of the kidneys offered matched the particular patient for whom they were volunteered. The kidneys were about to be wasted. All three patients were at the same hospital; and the doctors discovered that they could match each potential donor's kidney to one of the other two patients in the hospital. By doing all the transplants simultaneously—by taking advantage of **economies of scale** in performing transplants—the transplanting doctors were able to avoid wastage and produce the output, the transplants, more efficiently than had been possible before.

> *Q: Are study groups—a few students getting together twice a week to go over class material for your introductory economics class—an example like the one in this vignette? What are the similarities and differences?*

7.3

One of our friends sells real estate in town. She now advertises "virtual tours" on the Web of the houses that she is offering. This is not merely a gimmick to attract customers. In our house-buying episodes, we spent lots of time driving with the real-estate agent to houses and then quickly going through them. Many of these were houses that the realtor thought we might like but, in fact, failed completely to match our tastes. With the virtual tour, the agent can give us a list of houses to "tour" on the Web. We can rule out those that the agent thinks we'd like but that, in fact, are a poor match. This saves both of us huge amounts of time (and saves the agent gasoline, since she doesn't have to drive us around as much). The savings exceed her costs of constructing and maintaining the website. The **marginal product** of creating and maintaining this website is quite high.

> *Q: If you were the real-estate agent, how would you calculate the monetary value from constructing a website that did this for you? Given this calculation, how much would you be willing to pay someone to construct the Web site for you?*

7.4

February 14—I received a forwarded e-mail today listing twenty-two supposedly clever pickup lines by economists for Valentine's Day. One is "More of you is always better." This makes good sense in the context of production: If you love someone, more of that person should be better. The **marginal product** should always be positive. Another line on this list is "There is no **diminishing marginal productivity** with you." It's really hard to believe that there is never diminishing marginal productivity, even with one's spouse or lover. Eventually, even the greatest romance can benefit from a (brief) respite, a bit of time apart.

> *Q: Economists are famous for being brutally frank. If you have a really strong relationship, and only if that is true, try explaining the economics in this vignette to the person you are involved with.*

7.5

I left a stack of handouts containing a problem set by the door to the classroom today. Each student was supposed to pick one up. The problem was that, in the last three minutes before class started, the line of students waiting to pick up the handouts and walk through the entryway to the classroom was getting longer and longer. I had a brilliant idea—make two piles—and I did that. More students per minute were able to pick up the handout and walk into the classroom. With the addition of more of the variable input (piles of handouts), the output (students walking into class) increased. But despite my doubling the number of stacks, the number of students walking into class each minute didn't double. The reason is that there was a fixed input—the size of the entryway into the room. If I had added a third pile, the output might have increased further, but not by very much. Even in distributing handouts before class, the principle of **diminishing marginal productivity** (of number of stacks of handouts) seems to work, caused by the existence of a related input whose quantity is not changed.

> *Q: What would be the marginal product of making a tenth pile of handouts if I already had nine? Is it possible that it is negative (in terms of the output, number of students picking up the handout each minute)? If so, what should I do?*

7.6

Chicken and Chips. A newspaper story is headlined "Taiwan sacrifices animals so rain gods will help chip makers." There has been a drought near Taipei, and water is an essential input into computer chip manufacturing. (It takes more than silicon, chip-stamping machinery, and labor to make a chip.) With all other measures failing, government and industry officials sacrificed pigs, chickens, and ducks to the rain gods. This did generate a drizzle, but not nearly enough rain to reduce drought conditions. The question is, What is the **marginal product** of an additional chicken sacrificed? How many chickens should be sacrificed? Economic theory suggests that, as with any other input, the sacrifice of chickens will be characterized by **diminishing marginal productivity.** Therefore, if the sacrificed chickens produced only a drizzle, sacrificing still more chickens is not going to add much rain. Presumably, the authorities understood this economic principle, as they decided to give up on animal sacrifice as an input into chip production and rely instead on cloud seeding. Whether the marginal product of cloud seeding is any higher than the marginal product of another sacrificed chicken is unclear.

Q: If animal sacrifice would help, and if they had not yet sacrificed any cattle, would a cattle sacrifice be more or less helpful than another chicken, pig, or duck sacrifice? Why, or why not?

7.7

Just before class, my economics major students were laughing at a conversation they overheard between the instructor of the previous class and her student. The student said, "I really need a good grade in this class 'cause my GPA has to be high for me to get into grad school." My students were laughing because the grade in that particular class could not have had much of an effect on the senior's GPA. The student (it wasn't an economics class, thank goodness) did not distinguish **marginal** from **average.** The same thing happens among my intro students at least once a year. Someone tells me that unless he or she gets a B in my class, his or her GPA will be so low that he or she will be thrown out of the university. These students also don't seem to know marginal from average. Their average is low because of their previous bad grades. The marginal grade—what they get in my class—is not going to affect their GPAs very much.

Q: Calculate your grade in this class so far and assume that it will be your course grade. What will happen to your GPA after this class? Compare that to this class's grade (the marginal grade).

7.8

A colleague asked whether he should let his intermediate macro-economics class go to hear a lecture by Paul Krugman, *New York Times* columnist and economics professor at Princeton, who was talking about the Argentinean debt crisis on campus during his class hour. The topic was clearly relevant for a macro class, especially because the course currently covers international issues. This late in the semester, the **marginal product** of the professor's time with the students is diminishing rapidly. They've never heard Krugman before; and he is a good lecturer. The marginal productivity of time spent with him would be quite high. The students should go to Krugman's lecture instead of to class, and the colleague should give a brief quiz about that lecture to make sure the students didn't just sleep in.

    Q: Would the advice be any different if it were the second week of class? How should the advice depend on the quality of the instructor?

7.9

A story in *The Economist* reports a new technology that will create "smart labels," each of which could be attached to every individual product on a grocery store's shelves. For example, every box of Wheaties would have a smart label affixed to it. They would replace bar codes and would be useful to prevent pilferage and to signal the store's computers when the shelf was empty. The company that manufactures the product reports that it can produce the chips at 10 cents per item if it produces one billion a year, but at 5 cents per item if it produces ten billion a year. Its **average total cost** falls as output increases. Whether this is because **average variable cost** falls as output increases or whether total **fixed cost** is such a huge share of **total cost** is unclear from the story.

    Q: Given the description in the vignette, can you tell what happens to marginal cost as the company expands its output of smart labels?

Cost Minimization/Profit Maximization

7.10

I was waiting in line at the local post office. In this post office, you take a number and get called by the clerk when the number comes up on a screen in the main room. In addition to two clerks in the main room, there is a third clerk in a little office on the side. He can't see the screen, so whenever he finishes with a customer, he walks out, looks at the screen, and calls a number. He did this three times in the ten minutes that I waited, taking about fifteen seconds each time he walked out and back. I figure he must do this about sixty times a day, taking a total of fifteen minutes walking back and forth. That means he spends at least fifty hours a year wasting the U.S. Postal Service's time this way. If he earns $20 per hour, he is wasting $1,000 per year. It's not his fault, but for no more than $500, the Postal Service could install an extension screen in his little office. Purchasing this little bit of capital would enhance this clerk's productivity. The **marginal product** of this investment good surely would exceed its price.

Q: What if he did this only twenty times a day? Would it pay the U.S. Postal Service to install the extension screen then?

7.11

When I visited the casinos in Las Vegas in the mid-1980s, large numbers of people worked there walking through aisles around the gaming machines (slot machines, poker machines, etc.), making change for people (so they could shove more nickels, dimes, and quarters into the machines). On my visit in 2002, these people had almost disappeared. The reason is simple: The machines are now able to accept paper money and can distinguish ones, fives, tens, twenties, fifties, and even hundred-dollar bills. This technical change has sharply reduced the demand for the unskilled workers who used to offer change. With labor costs rising, the casinos have **substituted** toward using a technology that relies more on capital and less on labor.

Q: A third input in this industry is real estate—the space that the machines occupy. As the gains to being on the Strip in Las Vegas have increased, what do you expect has happened to the number of machines per square foot of space?

7.12

Every morning, the bedspread has to be put back onto our king-size bed. How to do this involves a *choice of technology*—in this case, between two different methods of accomplishing the task of making the bed. Method A involves my wife or me doing it alone; with Method B we do it together. With Method A, the person has to walk from one side of the bed to the other twice to pull up the spread partway on each side; with Method B we each stand on a side of the bed and pull the spread up together. The total labor in Method B is less. Since it requires less labor, and since we value the labor from each of us the same, Method B is the economically efficient technology in this case. Only if we decided that my wife's time is much more valuable than mine, or that my time is much more valuable than hers, would it pay to choose Method A.

> *Q: Let's say that it takes us three minutes if one of us makes the bed alone, but takes one minute if we use Method B and do it together. How much more valuable than mine would her time have to be to make it worthwhile to have me do the job alone? How does your answer change if she and I derive some pleasure from making the bed together?*

7.13

Weather has severely reduced the supply of natural vanilla, causing its price to quintuple. No one eats vanilla; it's an input into many foods, including, best of all, vanilla milk shakes. The huge price increase has led food manufacturers to do their best to **substitute** other inputs for vanilla in production. This includes increased purchases of very inexpensive artificial Chinese vanilla to use in place of the more expensive natural product. The rise in the price of natural vanilla has also spurred the development of genetically engineered bacteria that produce vanilla as a by-product. While the price of this new product is still high, it is falling, and if the price of natural vanilla remains high—if the supply of the natural product doesn't increase soon—vanilla users will start substituting toward the genetically engineered input, too.

> *Q: What does the rise in the price of natural vanilla do to the demand for chocolate as an input into ice cream?*

7.14

My wife and I bumped into each other while both trying to prepare breakfast. That's reminiscent of the saying "Too many cooks spoil the broth." Why should that be true? After all, if each cook's

marginal product is positive, the broth has to be getting better and better as more cooks are added. Implicitly, the proverb states that, at some point, the marginal product of an extra cook becomes negative, and if still more cooks are added, the quality of the broth gets worse and worse until it is spoiled. No **profit-maximizing** firm would ever get to this point, though: As soon as a cook's marginal product fell below what his or her wage was, the firm would stop hiring. Even when cooks are "free," as in your own kitchen, the proverb is correct in implying that no cook should ever be allowed to have a negative marginal product.

> *Q: Have you ever worked in an office or plant where total product seemed to decline when certain workers were present? Have you ever had roommates (or siblings) whose "help" on a task appeared to lower total output?*

7.15

A study examined the determinants of the grades of students in Economics I. The authors had data on each student's grade in the course, his or her SAT score, the number of hours per week spent studying economics, and the number of hours spent in class. This research viewed the student as a "factory," generating a grade in the course with inputs of ability (or at least SAT score) and time (spent in the two uses, studying and attending class). If each hour of the day is equally valuable and students are rational, the productivity of the last hour studying should be the same as the productivity of the last hour going to class. This didn't happen: The guys' last hour going to class was much more productive than was the last hour they studied. They could have improved their grades with no more work by studying a bit less and attending class a bit more. The women were the opposite. The **marginal product** of class attendance was zero for them: Their grades would have been just as high if they hadn't gone to class quite as often. A heartwarming additional finding was that, while higher SAT scores did raise the grades, the effect of a low SAT score could be offset by a few extra hours of study each week.

> *Q: If completing more homework assignments also raises your economics grade, what should be your rule about the effect on your grade of an extra hour spent doing homework assignments, compared with an extra hour spent studying or going to class?*

7.16

Outside speakers are one input into education that a university provides. My university paid $10,000 to Speaker A and $2,500 to Speaker B. Both received their market wages for giving speeches. Speaker A's audience contained 200 people, and so did Speaker B's audience. Speaker A's price per audience member was therefore $50, four times as much as the $12.50 that Speaker B cost per student. Like any firm, the university should be sure that the *ratio of marginal products of its inputs equals the ratio of their prices*. In this case, that means that the university should hope that Speaker A's benefit per student was four times that of Speaker B, since he cost four times as much per student. From what I've heard, Speaker A's **marginal product**—the value per student of the knowledge he imparted and the ideas he stimulated—was actually less than Speaker B's. The university could have done better by having Speaker B talk twice and not inviting Speaker A.

> *Q:*   *If the university could obtain Speaker C, who charges $500 and would attract 300 students, should it hire her or hire Speaker B?*

7.17

One of my colleagues is a real computer geek. When I visit him in his office, I see that he has two large plasma display screens in front of him, with various windows open on each. I remark that this is a highly unusual arrangement and ask him in particular why he just doesn't buy one larger screen. He could then display the same number of windows, and each would be as large as it now is. He says very simply that it is cheaper to purchase two separate displays, each seventeen inches, than to buy a single larger display that has the same viewing space. (He's right: That would have to be a twenty-four-inch display, which currently costs much more than two seventeen-inch displays.) Apparently, there currently are **diseconomies of scale** in the production of computer displays, making it cheaper to produce two smaller ones than one big one.

> *Q:*   *What my colleague ignores is that having two displays requires him to do some additional programming and to shift his gaze between monitors. How should these considerations affect his decision about buying monitors?*

7.18

Sometimes economic journalists write things that are so completely meaningless, even though they sound very important, that one has to laugh. That's true even of the very fanciest newspapers. A story about the airline industry's problems in the *New York Times*, March 25, 2003, stated, "The economic problems . . . $18 billion in losses . . . are mostly attributable to high cost and low **revenue**." The journalist states first that profits are negative (there are losses). Since profit equals revenue minus cost, claiming that high cost and low revenue are the causes of the problem shows nothing. It just restates that there is a problem—that profits are negative. The relevant question for shareholders in the airlines, for their employees, for their customers, and for the government is why costs are high, why revenues are low, and what can be done to lower cost and raise revenue.

> *Q: This is a tautology—the journalist is just restating the definition. Can you find other statements in the press, or that you make, that simply restate a definition in different terms?*

7.19

In "The Boxer," Paul Simon wrote and sang, "Still a man hears what he wants to hear and disregards the rest." In economics, we call this bounded rationality: Consumers maximize utility and producers maximize profits, but it doesn't pay them to process all the information that constantly assaults them. A firm will not make every little change that would be required if it responded to each change in its costs or technology. This is not just a matter of avoiding costly adjustments of production to short-run changes. Instead, these limits arise because it doesn't pay firms to obtain and analyze all the information that might be relevant to decision making. Instead, a **profit-maximizing** firm will devote its resources to analyzing the information that the managers believe is most important to making profits. The rest will be disregarded.

> *Q: Consider the nearest McDonald's. List changes that you think would cause it to alter its methods of operation. List others that would change its costs, but that it might not pay attention to.*

CHAPTER 8

The Firm in the Short Run— Fixed and Variable Costs

How Much to Produce

8.1

Who isn't tired of having his or her e-mail inbox clogged up with Viagra offerings, deals on mortgages, and other sales on items not mentionable in polite society? The fraction of e-mail accounted for by spam has been rising rapidly, to the point where in early 2004 spam accounted for over half of the e-mails in most inboxes. The solution might be using prices to give the spammers incentives to stop sending this junk. A company is offering to sell major mailers electronic encryption "stickers" that would be recognized by Internet service providers and would appear as such on the screen. Only these would get through generic spam filters. A sticker will cost one cent. That's not much; but if, for example, a Viagra seller snares only one customer for each 10,000 e-mails, unless the profits per customer are at least $100, the **marginal cost** of the electronic sticker exceeds the benefits of spamming. In that case it would not be profitable for the company to keep sending out this kind of nearly universally unwanted e-mail. End of spam.

Q: What would happen to the amount of spam e-mail if the stickers cost 10 cents each? 1 cent per dozen? Do you think that this proposal would be more or less effective than federal anti-spam regulations?

8.2

In the movie *Fight Club*, Edward Norton's character tells a fellow airplane passenger that he works as a "recall coordinator" for an automobile company and that the job is simple: "Multiply the size of the out-of-court settlement of a lawsuit times the number of cars times the probability of an accident. If less than [some level of cost] x, no recall." This expected value calculation is a good **profit-maximizing** strategy for a (heartless) car company if it doesn't care about risk. If it does, the policy leads to too few recalls: It ignores the chance that one big, although unlikely, lawsuit will bankrupt the company. It also ignores the possibility that enough bad publicity will lead consumers to demand fewer cars, costing the company **revenue** and reduced profits.

Q: Do you think that a small company would be more or less likely than a large company to be concerned about the kind of risk described here? Why, or why not?

8.3

Prices of color TVs in China are plummeting. The Chinese government essentially has guaranteed manufacturers in that country that their workers' wages will be paid no matter what the firm's **revenue** is. Workers' wages don't really cost the companies anything—the government has converted labor costs into a **fixed cost.** Firms can now cut prices and need only cover the relevant remaining costs—their **variable costs**—to still make a profit.

*Q: If labor costs become fixed costs, what are left as variable costs? Graph the typical firm's **average fixed cost** and **average variable cost** before and after labor costs are subsidized. Then answer the question: Why would these companies lower their prices to the point where their profits are negative?*

8.4

One of the teaching assistants from last semester's class came by my office asking me to write a recommendation for an internship he is seeking. I said I'd be happy to do so. He then asked if it would be OK if he used my name for other internships or jobs he might seek. I said, "Of course: The marginal effort required for additional recommendations is almost zero once I've written the first recommendation." He seemed a bit surprised by my reaction, but the **marginal cost** of writing more recommendations for the same student is tiny, since I have an electronic version of the letter on file. (The gain to him in terms of potential jobs is the same for each additional letter I write.)

Q: I always tell students to bring all recommendation requests to me at one time. How are the costs to me different compared with what they would be if I handled them one at a time?

8.5

A student who did very well in my principles class last semester came by to ask about other classes to take. After he received the usual advice, including an offer to steer him to the better teachers of economics, he flatteringly (and naively) asked if I teach all the courses in the curriculum. I chuckled and said no, of course not. The reason, I told him, is that teaching a course requires incurring large **fixed costs** of generating lecture materials and organizing notes. For that reason, I, like professors at every college and university, try to repeat courses as much as possible. By doing that, we can spread the fixed cost of generating the course over as many units of output (number of times teaching the class) as possible.

Q: Given my response, if you were a professor and had to teach four courses per semester, would you rather be in a faculty with five economics professors or one with forty economics professors? As a student, how do you think the quality of teaching differs if each professor is responsible for teaching all the courses in the curriculum, compared to a situation like the one I described in my response to the student?

8.6

A nursing home in town has more beds than it can currently fill. What its managers have done is use the nursing home bedrooms for assisted-living residents, senior citizens who do not need nursing care but can't live entirely on their own. The difficulty is that nursing patients pay much more than do assisted-living residents. The director of the home is upset about this and believes he is losing money on each assisted-living resident. He's right: He is losing money compared to his **average total cost,** but unless there is a list of nursing patients who would take the rooms and can pay the higher price, he should not worry about it.

While he is losing money on the existing people, he is more than covering all costs except the **fixed cost** that he already incurred when the building was constructed. If he threw the assisted-living residents out and left the rooms empty, he would lose the entire fixed cost.

Q: List some other fixed costs besides the costs of the building that make keeping the assisted-living residents even more advantageous for him.

8.7

The *Wall Street Journal* tells of jet-setters who are deserting South Beach (Miami, Florida) because the trendy clubs there have become less exclusive. How exclusive should a club be? Each club faces a **profit-maximizing** decision, just as firms do. So do professional associations that award honors to their members. If there is too little exclusivity, existing members will feel that belonging to the club is not worthwhile. Too many awards, and previous recipients feel their prize has been devalued. Each club or association should continue to admit people or give out awards until the marginal value to the association or club of having one more member or one more recipient of an award falls below the cost to the club in lost membership or in disgruntled prior winners of its awards.

Q: Apply the reasoning here to honorary societies at your high school or to a fraternity or sorority.

8.8

The local electric company is offering me a "free" fancy thermostat, one that is programmable for different times of day and days of the week. In return, I have to agree to let the company turn off the air conditioning for up to 10 minutes each half hour between 4 PM and 8 PM on the hottest summer days. Why is it giving this deal? The short-run marginal cost of producing electricity is very low—most times, the power plants are underutilized. They are fully utilized only at times of peak demand, including dinnertime. At those times, the **marginal cost** of producing electricity becomes huge, prompting power companies to buy expensive power from elsewhere or even to propose building new plants. If it can get consumers to cut back at these peak times, its **long-run average cost** will be reduced a lot, and it will make greater profits.

> *Q: How might the same idea be applied to tolls on local highways?*

8.9

The local specialized cardiac hospital is now advertising that it has reduced the price of a "Heart Saver CT (CAT scan)" from its usual $300 to only $100. It advertises, "This is a great way to make sure there are no signs of heart calcification building up which can cause heart problems later on." I am sure the hospital means well and wishes to prevent more serious heart disease, but economic considerations must have a lot to do with the decision to cut the price so drastically. First, the CAT scan machines are already in the hospital, are not fully utilized, and represent the majority **(fixed) cost** of the scan. The $100 is still above **marginal cost.** Second, this specialized hospital faces competition from a nearby general hospital that is trying to expand its cardiac unit. The Heart Hospital hopes to get patients and their doctors accustomed to the idea that this is the hospital of choice for any future cardiac problems.

> *Q: Assume that the $300 price covered the **average total cost** of giving a CT scan. What would have to be true about **average variable cost** for it to be sensible to offer the new lower price?*

8.10

Several of my statistics students complained today that they are having trouble finding a term paper topic. Finding a topic is equivalent to incurring a **fixed cost:** Until they've found a topic, they have nothing. Once they have decided on a topic, they are ready to incur the variable cost of finding data, thinking about the topic some more, doing the statistical work, and writing up the results into a term paper for the course. They—and any student—should think about writing assignments this way. This means that if the topic turns out to be a bad one, you should discard it before you sink more (time) costs into it. Also, spending immense amounts of time worrying about which topic to choose is irrational: By itself, those costs of searching have rapidly **diminishing**

marginal productivity, and until you actually start working on the project, you don't know if it will "pan out." Minimize the fixed cost of finding a topic by discarding unpromising topics. That way, you don't become wedded to what turns out to be a bad idea.

> *Q: Is the answer any different if you have three term papers in one semester? Does the existence of these fixed costs explain students' interest in using an expanded version of a term paper in two separate courses?*

8.11

I'm stranded at Denver Airport because my flight arrived so late that I missed my connection. Because the delay was caused by weather problems, the airline won't pay for a hotel room for me. But the ticket agent says: No problem, hotels near here will give you a room on an emergency basis for $36—and will give you a free ride from the airport to the hotel and back. This sounds great, and I wind up in a very nice hotel room on whose door the regular price is listed as $145. Why does the hotel offer such a cheap rate at the last minute, given that the **average cost** of a hotel room must be well above $36? The hotel room would otherwise be empty if not given to me at the last minute. Because the **marginal cost** of a room (cleaning, checking me in, and perhaps a few minor costs) is well below $36, the hotel loses less on the room by letting me occupy it than by letting it remain empty.

> *Q: Why doesn't the group of hotels in this scheme charge more than $36? I would be happy to pay somewhat more; and, since I am unlikely to be stranded again in Denver anytime soon, they don't need to worry about offending me and losing my future business.*

8.12

The Metropolitan Museum in New York City does not charge admission. But when you enter, there is a set of suggested contributions for visitors. The sign reads, "By paying the full $12 admission price you help defray the $34 per-person cost for each visitor." The $34 is clearly the **average cost** per visitor. I would think that the marginal cost of each additional visitor is well below $12. The admission more than covers **marginal cost** but far from covers average cost. By keeping the museum full of visitors (and it was mobbed on a Friday morning in a nonvacation week),

THE FIRM IN THE SHORT RUN—FIXED AND VARIABLE COSTS   97

its managers can at least recoup some of the costs of keeping it open.

Q: Graph the cost curves for the Metropolitan Museum. Does the average total cost slope up or slope down, or is it flat?

8.13

The guy on the elliptical trainer next to me at 5:30 AM today asked whether I have teaching assistants (TAs) in my large micro principles class. I said yes (and thought that the production process requires my labor and TA labor—we're the human inputs into production). Between gulps for air, he then asked, "How many TAs?" I am typically offered five TAs to help with the 500 students in the class. The problem is that the **marginal products** of the fourth and fifth TAs are low. They're low both because of the way I organize my grading and exams and because the marginal TAs assigned to me are typically new and inexperienced graduate students. On the cost side, I don't pay any money for the TAs, but the more TAs I have, the more time and effort I must spend coordinating their activities and supervising them. Worse still, the required effort rises very rapidly as the number of TAs rises. So with declining **marginal "revenue"** and rising **marginal "cost,"** I don't want all five TAs. I just thank the department chairman and tell him that three good TAs are enough to do the job just fine.

Q: In many universities, a "head TA" supervises an army of TAs for the professor who does the lecturing. As a student, how do you feel about this? Is this a gain in the "output" of the course? Does it result in improved learning for you, the student?

The Firm's Shut-Down Point

8.14

I went into a video store in Minneapolis late in 2002 to rent a DVD for my parents' new DVD player. The store, a small independent operation, contained only VHS cassettes; and the owner seemed somewhat insulted when I asked if he carried DVDs. How could this guy stay in business without renting out DVDs? Surely, with the explosion of DVD players, the demand for his goods was down. (At least mine was down—I walked out immediately.) The **fixed cost** of the cassettes that he had bought had already been incurred. All he needed to do was cover the **average variable cost** of his operation—rental on the store and his time. So even if his demand was reduced, he could still make enough money to remain in business. Eventually, and surely as more old movies are released in DVD, he would either have to start stocking DVDs or find his demand is so low that he couldn't even cover variable cost, at which point he would have to close down. Sure enough, by summer 2004, the store was closed. The owner apparently must have continued his policy against stocking DVDs; and so few customers were interested in renting VHS cassettes that he must not even have been able to cover his variable cost.

Q: DVD players were widespread for at least five years before this store closed. Why did it take so long for the store to become unprofitable?

8.15

Last night, my wife made dough to bake *rugelach,* a Jewish baked delicacy sort of like cinnamon twists. This morning, she announced to me that she mistakenly used whole-wheat flour and doesn't think the treats will be as good as usual. She says, "I haven't done the time-consuming work yet, so I think I'll throw out the dough and start over again tonight." This decision requires a conscious balancing of benefits and costs. The benefit of throwing out the dough is that the final product will taste somewhat better, but she will have to incur the **fixed cost** (making the dough, this time with white flour) again. The scary thought is: What if she had already rolled out and twisted the treats? Would she then have gone ahead and baked them, knowing that they would not be as good as usual? How bad would they have had to be if she had already rolled and twisted the dough before she threw everything away and started again?

Q: Have you ever done an experiment for a biology or chemistry class where you knew you made a mistake early on and had to decide whether to continue? What did you do then? What would you have done if you had made the mistake further along in the experiment?

8.16

It's a Sunday evening in June in the tourist section of Moscow, Russia, not far from Red Square. It's 9 PM and still quite light out at this very far northern latitude. Amazingly enough, the stores, such as Burberry, Cerruti, and others that cater to tourists and rich Russians, are open. This seems to make no sense—how much are they going to sell at this time of day and on Sunday? In fact, it makes a lot of sense. Most of the costs of operating the store are **fixed costs**—the land, the inventory, and so on. The only **variable cost** is labor and power, both of which are relatively inexpensive in today's Russia, especially compared to the price of land in downtown Moscow and to the prices of the goods that these stores sell. That being the case, the stores don't have to sell much at this time of day to cover their variable costs and make additional profits.

 Q: OK, so why don't these stores stay open 24 hours a day?

8.17

Universities offer summer school classes for a variety of reasons. I hope when my university offers a class in the summer that the people doing the planning are thinking economically. The university has a fixed plant that will sit idle if it is not used in the summer. The university thus shouldn't worry about the **fixed cost** of the buildings, but **variable costs** are still important. The professor's salary and fringe benefits are extra costs that wouldn't be incurred if he or she were not teaching the course. The building must be cooled (no small issue in Texas in August), and lighting must be provided. Also, the extra cost of registering the students for the summer must be paid. If the tuition payments of the students who signed up for a summer class don't cover these variable costs, the university should think carefully about whether to offer the course. If it offers the course at a tuition that doesn't even cover variable cost, the university is choosing to subsidize students to attend summer school.

 *Q: Say the professor's salary and benefits for teaching the course are $5,000, the extra electricity for air-conditioning and lighting costs $500, and the extra cost of registering the students in the class is $50. How much tuition **revenue** will have to be received to justify offering the course? Given what tuition charges per course are at your college or university, how many students need to sign up for the course to make it worthwhile for your school to offer it?*

8.18

I run long-distance or work out in the gym, trying to avoid doing the same thing two days in a row. This morning I went to the gym at 5:30 AM, but it wasn't open yet even though it was scheduled to be open then. I stood in line for ten minutes, and it still hadn't opened. Should I wait around or go home and go for a run? Remembering lectures about the firm in the short run, I realized that **fixed cost** (the time I had already spent) shouldn't matter. I assumed that it would be a while before the gym opened, and since I had neither run nor worked out yesterday and had only a limited time left to exercise, I left the line and went home for a run.

> *Q: How should my reaction (or yours if you were in this situation) differ if I had exercised every day for the previous three days? What if I had been unable to exercise for a week? Why the difference?*

8.19

A lot of the musical events that my wife and I go to are on work-days. By the time the show starts at 8 PM, we're pretty tired after a full day's work. By the intermission, we say to ourselves, "Why stay for the second half? We've gotten a lot of enjoyment already, the marginal enjoyment is small, and we're exhausted." None-theless, most times we stay. You would think we would realize that we would view the prior purchase of the ticket as a **fixed cost** that shouldn't matter to us, yet it does. This is quite common behavior. While businesses may think only about the dollars in their mar-ginal decisions, people have more than just dollars in their utility functions. Having already spent the money, we have a mental com-mitment to the entire show and will stay even though a simple marginal consideration that looks only at future costs (in this case, our increasingly valuable time) and benefits (the remainder of the show) would lead us to go home at intermission.

> *Q: Why even buy the ticket, knowing that it is likely that we will be ready to leave at intermission yet will feel we have to stay?*

8.20

Vignette 2.4 refers to a very long movie that was boring right from the start and that continued to be boring. We went to that movie on New Year's Eve, a night when we had planned to see the movie then go out partying. After one hour, we were ready to give up on the movie and leave the theater, having wasted our money on the $7 tickets. Being an economist, I said: "Let's wait, it's almost over. Our tickets are a **fixed cost,** but the remaining

variable cost must be tiny, since the movie can't last more than forty-five minutes more." After another forty-five minutes, we debated leaving and again decided that the remaining variable cost—the time left in the movie—had to be small. This happened two more times, resulting in our enduring three and a half hours of boredom. We hadn't ignored the nature of fixed cost. Rather, we kept on underestimating how large were the variable costs (of staying longer in the theater). We weren't irrational, just badly informed about the length of the movie.

Q: What if we had known how long the movie was right from the start and had paid $20 for the movie tickets? What should we have done after one hour?

8.21

Deciding how to read this book requires an economic decision. Biological studies of learning suggest that people learn better if they spread the same total amount of time over more individual sessions. "Cramming" for exams is not as good a way to learn as is steady studying done regularly during the semester. For example, ten times the marginal gain from reading two pages of this book at one sitting exceeds the marginal gain from reading twenty pages at one sitting. So why not read the book in two-page units? Each two-page reading session requires you to decide to begin the book, drop your other activities, pick up the book, open it, and so forth. While the benefits from this approach exceed those from cramming the book, the **fixed costs** of this approach are so large that it is not a sensible economic decision. Most people will make the smart economic decision to read the book chapter by chapter, even though they'd learn more by reading just a few vignettes at a time.

Q: Compare this book to your math textbook. Are the fixed costs of studying this book regularly higher or lower than those for the math book? Are the gains to regular study, compared to cramming, higher or lower? What do these considerations tell you about how you should study the two given the scarcity of your time?

8.22

This One Is for the Birds. Texas has been the home of the boom in emu ranching. In the late 1980s and early 1990s, there was a speculative boom in emus, the Australian equivalent of ostriches.

Prices for eggs and chicks skyrocketed as ranchers foresaw that emus might replace cattle as a cash crop. Unfortunately, while a small market for emuburgers was created, the price of a breeding pair of emus had fallen by the late 1990s from $4,500 to $20. The supply of emus was huge, and there was little demand. What is an emu rancher to do? The **variable cost** of raising an emu to slaughter weight—the cost of feeding the emu—was less than the price of a mature bird. Not surprisingly, smart farmers simply released their emus into the wilds of Texas. The local paper headlined "Abandoned emus run amok on Texas roads," and several of the flightless birds wound up being hit by cars at night on rural roads.

Q: How high would the price of adult emus have to be to lead farmers to raise chicks to maturity?

8.23

The city of Austin recently began marketing bottled water under its own special label. The water is just tap water that the city pays to have taken by truck to Dallas (nearly 200 miles away), bottled, and then shipped back to be marketed in Austin. The **average total cost** of a case of 24 bottles is $8.90, while the city sells a case for only $6. It thus loses $2.90 on each case that it sells. The city has decided to stop marketing the water. Is this a wise decision? It probably is: It is hard to believe that **average fixed cost** is as high as $2.90 a case—the major costs appear to be variable and arise from the bottling, shipping, and distribution of the water. **Average variable cost** is almost certainly above $6, meaning that the city is losing money on every case it sells. What's amazing is not that the city is stopping production, but that, knowing the price and cost structure, the city ever got into the business in the first place.

Q: Let's say the average fixed cost currently is $2. How should the city's decision about whether or not to stay in the bottled water business be affected if it could get fixed cost down to $1 per case?

8.24

Luke 13:6–9 recognizes **opportunity cost, fixed cost,** and **variable cost:** "A certain man had a fig tree . . . and said unto the dresser of his vineyard, Behold, these three years I come seeking fruit on this fig tree, and find none: cut it down; why cumbereth it the ground? And he answering said unto him, Lord, let it alone this year also, till I shall dig about it, and dung it; and if it bear fruit, well; and if not, then after that thou shalt cut it down." The dresser realizes that the fixed cost (the three barren years) that annoy the owner have gone by. He also knows that the land has a positive opportunity cost—another tree can be planted there. He believes, though, that incurring a bit more variable cost (the digging and dunging) might have a high **marginal product** (lots of figs), and that this **marginal cost** is worth paying, but only for one year. After a year, he assumes that the marginal cost of another year of dunging and digging is not going to make the tree more productive, and the tree should be cut down.

Q: *How would the dresser of the vineyard have responded if the fig tree had been barren for nine years? Why might his answer have been different even though both three years and nine years of barrenness would represent fixed cost?*

8.25

Most of the snow-cone stands in Austin close in mid-October, once the ninety-degree-plus days have disappeared and the demand for snow cones becomes small. At that point, it doesn't pay a company to incur the **variable costs** of keeping the stands in operation. But the company that has shut down still has the **fixed cost** of renting the stand that is sitting idle. One of the owners found a solution: He switched the snow-cone stand to a taco stand! The demand for tacos is higher in the winter in Austin than in the summer, so the owner can spread the fixed costs of the stand over more months, thus lowering **average total cost** for the year and making higher profits. This is a clever way of handling the problem of seasonal variations in demand for a product.

Q: *List two businesses that you know of that close down in the winter. How could each of them adapt to a different product that could be marketed in winter so that the owner could spread the fixed cost?*

8.26

A local bakery advertises that it is open from 9 AM to 6 PM on Saturdays. But at 4:45 PM today, signs on its door read "Sold out" and "Closed." Is this a sensible policy, not having enough baked goods to allow the store to remain open each day for the listed hours? Yes. The baker does not know how demand fluctuates from day to day. If she always baked enough—if she incurred the fixed cost of baking a huge amount every day—there would be leftovers on most days that would be wasted or sold at very low prices. To run out once in a while is better than regularly to incur the costs of producing goods that will not be sold. But if she runs out on many days and at random times of the day, customers will stop coming. On most days, fluctuating demand will ensure that there will be leftovers even at 6 PM.

> *Q: How would the baker's decision about how much to bake each morning change if the amount of day-to-day fluctuations in demand increased? How would the number of days on which she closed early change?*

CHAPTER 9

*C*ompetitive Markets in the Long Run

Equilibrium

9.1

We just rented a house in Stone Harbor, New Jersey, for a week next summer. Stone Harbor is a long, narrow island, with the west side on a saltwater inlet and the east side on the Atlantic Ocean, with First Avenue nearest the ocean and Third Avenue nearest the bay. Bayfront rentals are slightly more expensive than those for houses nearer to Third Avenue, and prices stay the same until you get fairly close to First Avenue moving eastward. After that, the rentals skyrocket, with the price for oceanfront rentals being three times that of rentals between Second and Third Avenues. Why is the price in **competitive equilibrium** for an oceanfront rental so very much higher when one can walk to the ocean beach from Third Avenue in less than ten minutes?

> *Q: Give an answer for this question—if you can. Is it that the ocean view is so highly valued? Is it prestige? What do you think will happen to the difference in rental prices between the houses near the ocean and those farther away as the number of people wanting to spend time in Stone Harbor expands?*

9.2

The economics editor of a major commercial textbook publisher mentioned a very interesting problem facing his company. They sell an increasing share of their books internationally. The profit on those books is much lower than the profit on domestic sales. Competing textbooks that are printed abroad are of much lower quality, with inferior paper and fewer colors. To compete with these books when it sells to international wholesalers, his company must charge a low price. He then mentioned a problem in a related market: The used textbook market in the United States has been growing. He and his colleagues believe this has occurred partly because international buyers buy up used copies of the low-priced textbooks that originally were sold abroad. They then ship them back to the United States, where they are resold at the high price in the U.S. market for used books. The original publisher finds the market for new books in the United States undercut, but has made only very low profits from the international market. The solution, so he claimed only half jokingly, is a textbook that self-destructs after one use. Only that way can low-**average-cost** products be excluded from the market.

> *Q: If this publisher's analysis is correct and the market for new U.S. textbooks here is trimmed, what does this behavior do to the amount that publishers are willing to pay to textbook authors? What will happen to the supply of new textbooks?*

9.3

A good detective typically has good economic sense. In Ian Rankin's *The Hanging Garden* (New York: St. Martin's Press, 1998), two detectives notice a shop near a warehouse that they believe to be a target for a gang of robbers. The heroic detective says, "The usual ploy with a shop like that is to take a beating on one or two necessities to get the punters [suckers] in [to buy expensive items]. But that place looked like Bargain City." He then tells his colleague to investigate the shop. He believes that, if a competitive firm seems to be losing money on all the items it sells, the only way it can operate is if some other activity subsidizes its losses. In this case, the gang that is using the store to case out the target must be expecting to cover the store's losses with the gains that it expects from robbing the warehouse.

> *Q: Might the store be losing money on all items for a little while? If so, how can the detective be sure that he is right?*

9.4

A number of stories recently described "instant dates," a "market" in which single women are seated at a long table and single men sit down for a three-minute date with a woman. At the end of the three minutes, each party makes a note of whether he or she would be interested in seeing the other again. The men then move on to the next woman, and so on, so that each person meets roughly thirty new people in a single evening. Dating can be viewed as the information-gathering activity in the competitive market for spouses. It's a way that we can find out about other people and how well they match us and we match them. It is very time-consuming at a period of life when the value of time is increasing rapidly. The instant date reduces the time costs of gathering information and makes the dating market work more efficiently. It may be a bit crude, but it is hard to argue that the instant date is more crude than singles bars, and it is much more efficient.

> *Q: Another market uses the same idea, but has eight-minute dates. What are the relative advantages and disadvantages of using the three-minute instant date market compared to the eight-minute instant date market? Which do you think is preferable?*

9.5

I always thought that miniature golf was a product of the 1950s, but it started in 1927 and spread like wildfire all over the United States. Entry was easy, and the profits obtained from the first courses built were enormous. What followed is standard in competitive industries. Attracted by huge potential profits, entrepreneurs built immense numbers of courses, usually quite cheaply and with little distinguishing one from another. As the growth of demand slowed and the market became saturated, most of the courses were soon losing money, and large numbers went out of business. Today the industry has stabilized, partly because the demand is more stable. Partly, too, higher entry costs have changed the business: Except for a few purists, most people today insist on waterfalls, mechanized swinging windmills, plastic gorillas, and other hazards that raise the cost of entering the market.

> *Q: What if someone invented an automatic scorekeeper to be installed on miniature golf courses? How would that change the market, including the size of the industry and the equilibrium price per game played?*

9.6

The Barbie doll has long been one of the premier toys in America and even beyond. The price has been very high. (We recently purchased Cowgirl Barbie for $20.) This has created large profits for Barbie's manufacturer, Mattel Corporation. Given the cost of production and marketing, the prices have always seemed un-usually high—much higher than could be sustainable in the long run in a competitive market. In the past few years, the prices of Barbie have fallen tremendously. Other manufacturers are now making dolls that are the same size as Barbie and that can wear Barbie's clothes. Apparently, the main attraction of the doll is not the Barbie face, but rather the ability to dress Barbie up. This has caused the prices of Barbie to plummet—in summer 2003, I was told that you can buy some Barbie dolls for as little as $4.99. Competition has driven the price down much closer to **long-run average cost.**

Q: Why might it have taken so long before companies entered the market and reduced Mattel's economic profits on Barbies to zero?

9.7

Russia is slowly privatizing the property that had been owned by the government in the Soviet days. The sell-off was rapid in the mid-1990s, but has been much slower and steadier since then. One of the reasons is that the citizens feel that the prop-erty was given away at ridiculously low prices to friends of the then-government. Does it matter? After all, that's just a transfer of wealth from the citizens to some political cronies who be-came very rich. It does matter in the long run, because it is not clear that the cronies are those who are most capable of using the resources most productively. Had the government auc-tioned the properties off openly, the highest bids would have been from those individuals and corporations who believed they would be able to use the assets to generate the greatest profits—the greatest surplus. There is no reason to think that the cronies are able to use the assets most productively. The loss was not just a one-time transfer of wealth from the people to the newly rich—it represents a continuing loss of output to society until the cronies sell the assets to those who are able to use them most efficiently.

Q: If the cronies are not efficient operators of the assets, what should they do: hold the assets or sell them? If they sell them and bidding for the assets is competitive, will the cronies benefit or lose?

9.8

University fund-raising offices contract with private telemarketers to phone alumni who previously have not donated to the university. The university typically pays a fixed fee, and the company guarantees the university that a certain amount will be raised. What incentives does the company have to work more than enough to raise anything extra beyond the guaranteed amount? There are many suppliers of these services; the market is competitive, and each supplier would like to retain the contracts it now has and obtain others. If it barely raises the guaranteed amount, the company hurts its reputation and will lose existing customers or at least fail to attract new ones. What incentives does the university have to avoid giving the company only the most difficult alumni? Same thing—if the university gives the company the worst prospects, companies soon learn to insist on higher fixed fees and/or lower guarantees to the university. Competition, through the need to maintain a reputation, forces both parties to be honest and leads to fees and guarantees that are dictated by the costs of offering the service.

Q: Some universities do all their fund-raising through telemarketers. Would the fixed fee in those cases be higher or lower than it is among schools that provide telemarketers only the names of those who have not previously donated? Would the guarantee by the company be higher or lower?

9.9

Casinos operated by Indian tribes have expanded tremendously nationwide in the last twenty years, with some turning into billion-dollar businesses. More recently, corporate-run casinos have expanded beyond Nevada and Atlantic City to a number of southern states. The Indian casinos are not liable to federal regulations on wages and working conditions. This gives them a competitive advantage over other casinos, since they can operate with lower labor costs and, thus, lower **long-run average cost.** The only way the other casinos can survive is by offering inferior payouts (retaining more of the money that is wagered) and hoping that not all their potential customers are lost to the Indian casinos.

> *Q: One state has both Indian and non-Indian casinos, while another has only non-Indian casinos. In which state are the non-Indian casinos more likely to survive?*

The Role of Market Size

9.10

In 1776, Adam Smith wrote in *The Wealth of Nations*, "The division of labor is limited by the extent of the market." One implication is that the bigger the market, the more room for specialized products. The applicability of this statement to a big city such as Austin, Texas, was made clear this morning. A pickup truck had a sign advertising www.dogduty.citysearch.com and saying that it belonged to Dog Duty Inc. The company offers to scoop things up from your lawn for $9 weekly for up to two dogs. This kind of specialized service couldn't exist in a smaller town because the sellers of the service wouldn't have enough business to occupy them on a full-time basis. But in a big town, the **market demand curve** is far enough to the right—and enough people are willing to pay the high price necessary to get someone to perform this fairly unpleasant task for them—that the company can survive and even prosper.

> *Q: Why might this company be able to offer its services at a lower price than a company that combines this service with lawn mowing or landscaping?*

9.11

Monterey, California, is very cold today, so we go into a clothing store to buy something warm. We find a real deal—only $12.99 for a PolarFleece pullover. But an additional sign states that the pullover costs $1 extra for size XXL. The large size uses more material, so it must be more costly to produce. But that's true for XL pullovers compared to L pullovers, for L compared to M, and so on. Why doesn't the company charge higher prices for each larger size generally? After all, Burger King charges more for a Whopper than for a Whopper Junior. If they don't, and the bigger ones cost more to produce, it means that size M people are paying a price above **average total cost,** while big people are paying a price below average total cost. The reason must be that pricing the different sizes differently is too costly for manufacturers and wholesalers, as is marking and advertising separate prices on each item distinguished by size for stores. Some distinctions can be made; for the few pieces of very large clothing, separate prices may make sense. Beyond that, incurring the costs of listing many prices, putting more complex programs in cash registers, and so on, just isn't worthwhile.

> *Q: If manufacturers started pricing each different size differently, would retail stores start charging differently by size?*

9.12

A woman who is planning her daughter's wedding said that the members of the bridal party were buying their dresses at a local branch of a national bridal chain store. The bridesmaids are scattered all over the United States, and that way they can be sure to get matching dresses. Nationwide bridal chain stores are a natural response to a more cosmopolitan and mobile population. If the members of each bridal party lived in the same town, nationwide chains would have no advantage other than perhaps being able to obtain volume discounts from manufacturers. With people living all over the country, nationwide chains have the additional long-run cost advantage of offering a product that will be used in only one location, but that is guaranteed to be identical in style no matter where it is purchased.

> *Q: Consider a different example. The Holiday Inn motel chain used to advertise "The best surprise is no surprise," thus pointing out the sameness of its motels all over the United States. Is the success of the sameness, and the advantage it gave large motel chains, caused by the underlying demand forces characterizing the growth of nationwide bridal shops? Or is there something else that makes the large motel chains so attractive to travelers?*

9.13

What's an efficient size for a church or synagogue? If there were **economies of scale** throughout, with all the Baptists in a big Texas city such as Austin, we'd see just one giant Baptist church.

With 10,000 Jews in Austin, we'd see just one big synagogue. We don't: There are many churches in each denomination, as well as many synagogues. As the city has expanded, more and more different kinds of Baptist churches, Jewish synagogues, and other churches have been organized. It's not just that each one serves a local area. People drive a long way to the church or synagogue of their choice even when another one is closer. They like the peculiarities of a leader's ministry, the type of service, and even the particular social interactions of a congregation. With one big house of worship, these choices would be lost. Statistical studies of the long-run average cost curves of churches suggest that this is true: There are economies of scale up to some size, but as the church or synagogue begins growing beyond a certain size, **diseconomies of scale** set in—it becomes less efficient.

> *Q:*   *What would cause diseconomies of scale eventually to show up in churches and synagogues? List some of the cost and production factors that limit the growth of an individual church or synagogue.*

CHAPTER 10

Competitive Markets— Responses to Shocks

Changes in Technology and Costs

10.1

I made some international air reservations over the Web today. In the past, the airlines offered travel agents an 8 percent commission on tickets booked by an agent, with the airlines taking the commission out of the price of the ticket. These commissions have been decreasing and in many cases have been abolished, since the travel agents must now compete with the automation of the Web. The problem is that the labor costs incurred by the travel agents necessitate at least some minimum commission. Travel agencies cannot cover costs with commissions much lower than the current ones. The new **competitive equilibrium** in response to this technical change—the development of a substitute, cheap method of booking tickets—is that the reduced number of people who cannot or do not wish to book their own tickets are still using travel agents, and the travel agencies are now charging commissions to those clients to cover the agencies' costs. Travelers who are capable of booking fares on the Web are doing so, and the actual Web fare is lower than the cost of a ticket bought through an agency. Even the airlines themselves have, as of summer 2004, started behaving this way: Now several airlines require an extra fee to book via telephone with them if you do not want to book over the Web.

> *Q: This vignette describes what eventually will be a new competitive equilibrium in this market. Graph the initial **long-run average cost** curve before the use of the Web to book travel. Then graph the new curve and show how the equilibrium has changed.*

10.2

I spent three hours a few days ago taking part in a teleconference—a meeting of about 10 people that took place by conference call. This group used to meet face-to-face three times a year, but this year we decided to do one of the three meetings by teleconference. This is apparently increasingly common: *The Economist* reports that face-to-face meetings in 2001 before September 11 constituted over 50 percent of all meetings, while in 2004 they were only 40 percent. No doubt the hassles of air travel after September 11 explain part of this. But surely part is also due to the producers (people who schedule meetings) substituting relatively less expensive inputs into production. They can use ever-falling telephone rates instead of airline tickets and avoid wasting people's increasingly valuable time traveling to meetings when they can use that time doing something else. This substitution doesn't work for all meetings, as our choice to do this only once a year shows; but it is increasingly a cost-saving way of conducting business.

> *Q: Graph the average cost curves before and after September 11 for meetings of national organizations; then for meetings of state organizations; then for meetings of local organizations. Where do you expect the biggest change to have taken place?*

10.3

A fifty-inch wall-hanging flat-screen television is priced around $8,000 today at retail. How much will it cost in 2008? Increased competition will drive the price down. Also, as companies produce more of them, they should be able to take advantage of **economies of scale.** The price will drop a lot, perhaps even below $2,000, by then.

> *Q: Go back and find the price of a DVD player in a newspaper advertisement from 1998 and compare it to prices today. Do the same thing for a seventeen-inch CRT monitor in 1998 compared to today. Do these changes represent movements along **long-run average cost** curves, or do they represent technical changes that have shifted the long-run average cost curves downward?*

10.4

I taped a video on the costs of traffic accidents for Defensive-Driving.com. This new company is licensed to provide online instruction in safe driving for people who wish to avoid paying traffic tickets and reduce the penalty points on their driver's licenses. Until its inception, bad drivers had to attend classes in person. They bore the cost of the time spent driving to and from the defensive driving school and doing so at possibly inconvenient times. Also, the providers had to rent space large enough to accommodate their "students." The new technology has thus both lowered the **average total cost** of providing the service and has made it more attractive to "students." Not surprisingly, business for the new online company is booming—it can undercut its live competitors.

> *Q: Why isn't Web-based college education replacing in-person college education as rapidly as it is in this example?*

10.5

A student mentioned her family's business, a small pet store. Her parents emigrated from Korea in the early 1980s and started this store in Houston. The business prospered for a while, but in the 1990s things started to go badly. The reason is that a PETsMART outlet opened nearby. PETsMART and one or two other pet superstore chains expanded tremendously during that period. **Economies of scale** in inventorying and purchasing have increased the efficient scale for production in the retail pet industry. This happened many years ago in the grocery business and in some other retailing, but it is recent in this industry. Her parents are the unfortunate victims of a change in technology that has changed the **competitive equilibrium.**

> *Q: Draw the **long-run average cost** curves describing this industry in the early 1980s. Then show how they changed in the 1990s.*

10.6

Michael Lewis's book *Moneyball* (Norton, 2003) is a description of how the recruitment of amateur players into professional baseball changed from being done on a "seat-of-the pants" basis to a somewhat scientific approach. It describes how the general manager of the Oakland Athletics, Billy Bean, innovated by using a more scientific approach to selecting players. The technological change in choosing players came about because the benefits of adopting the new technology rose: With players' salaries averaging more than ten times what they had been in the 1970s, the benefits from choosing players more correctly (or, obversely, the loss arising from choosing a bad player) increased proportionately. At the same time the growth of personal computers, and the increasingly widespread knowledge of how to analyze statistics, lowered the costs of acquiring and processing the information that would allow baseball general managers to make better choices about player recruitment.

Q: Per dollar spent on player salaries, the Oakland A's have one of the top two records in the major leagues. Most other teams don't use their methods, relying instead on "seat-of-the pants" approaches to choosing players. Why hasn't the demonstrated value of the A's approach caused others to adopt it?

10.7

Denmark is the leading exporter of pork products in Europe. In the early 1980s, the typical Danish pig farmer produced 200 pigs per year. Presumably, the farmers of the time were efficient—they were operating at the minimum of the **long-run average cost curve** given the technology of the 1980s. That scale of operation wouldn't be competitive today. Technology has changed so that today's Danish pig farmer produces more than 1,500 porkers per year; the minimum of the long run average cost curve has shifted far to the right. **Economies of scale** now cover a much broader range of production in this industry than they did in the 1980s, requiring the surviving pig farms to become larger in order to survive.

Q: Draw the long-run average cost curve for the early 1980s and for now. What do you think has happened to the number of pig farmers in Denmark, and why?

10.8

Our younger son got us to watch *The Iron Chef* on the Food Channel on his cable television service. The show is apparently a cult favorite with college students, some of whom, so it is said, get extra pleasure from watching it while smoking outlawed substances. This show could never have been on national television when I was in college. There were only three national networks in those days. To be profitable, a television show had to appeal to a very broad national audience. The change in technology that was brought about by cable transmission has greatly increased competition among suppliers of entertainment. It has lowered the breakeven point for a television show's audience and given television a much greater ability to cater to the tastes of small groups of viewers.

> *Q: Satellite television allows you to view television broadcasts from all over the world. How will this affect the breakeven point in the United States for TV shows?*

10.9

Many years ago most American hospitals and other medical institutions had self-contained food-service units, with the entire operation done by the hospital's own employees. Today, an increasing number of hospitals contract out to large food-service organizations to provide meals to patients and to staff. Why the change? My doctor friends suggest it is a combination of **economies of scale** and changing technology and related prices. The price of a day in a hospital has increased very rapidly over the past twenty years. At the same time, medical people have recognized that good nutrition, including providing food that patients find palatable, helps get patients home faster. Hospitals have an increased incentive to use organizations that have the know-how to provide decent nutrition and tasty food, something the hospitals' own staff couldn't do as well. This creates a competitive advantage for the large food-service companies where none had previously existed.

> *Q: Would the effect commented on in this vignette be more or less likely to occur in a hospital in a major metropolitan area or in a small rural hospital?*

10.10

Our favorite movie theater complex, which has seven theaters and is only three miles from our house, is closing next month. Its closing means that twenty-seven movie screens will have shut down in the last four years in a radius of five miles of our house. In the story about the closing, one local movie buff complained, "Regrettably, it's all about economics." I agree, and the economics has to do with the growing importance of **economies of scale** in the operation of movie complexes. Except for a very few art houses and specialty theaters (two in my town serve pizza and drinks while you watch a movie sitting on benches with tables in front of you), smaller complexes are shutting down.

> *Q: Draw the **long-run average cost** curves in the movie theater business before and after the changes that have generated the new equilibrium in movie theater complexes.*

10.11

There's a big crisis in home insurance in Texas. Insurers are refusing to cover homeowners for mold damage. Recently, this has engendered many large lawsuits, costing the insurers unexpected settlements. Nobody knows what the risks from the mold might be or how big the damages it causes could become. Insurance doesn't work when the insurers can't assess the risks: The market breaks down, and there is now no **competitive equilibrium** price at which insurance can be bought. Only after the level of risk is more certain can the market be reestablished.

> *Q: This is what economists call a "lemons problem": Uncertainty about quality in this case is so great that no one is willing to supply the product. If you were working for an insurer, could you even draw an **average total cost** curve for your product?*

Shifts in Industry Demand

10.12

Drove by a drive-in movie theater today—and, of course, it was long-since closed. There were nearly 5,000 drive-in theaters in the United States in the 1950s. Today, there are fewer than 1,000. Why? This is a case where the **average cost curve** rose a lot, while average cost in competing industries fell relatively. The land the drive-ins were built on became more valuable; drive-ins take a lot of land, while movie multiplexes take much less per customer. The drive-ins were also hit by a leftward **shift in the demand curve.** Hearing the movie through a speaker hanging on the window of your car wasn't so bad when the sound in movie theaters wasn't good, but it couldn't compete against Dolby and THX Surround Sound. Finally, as any suburban teenager in the 1950s knew, drive-ins were attractive on dates for other reasons; and with looser attitudes in the 1960s, the demand for drive-in movies declined, too.

> *Q: Numerous drive-through stores that sell beer had been gasoline stations until the 1970s, when the price of gasoline skyrocketed. How is this switch analogous to that described here? What use can be made of old drive-in movie sites?*

10.13

The last dairy farmer in Travis County (the county where Austin, Texas, is located) is closing down his farm. "I'm tired of losing money," he said, citing declining milk prices, competition from large commercial dairies, and increasing property taxes due to rising land values. What are the implications of his closing for how cost curves shift and how firms enter and/or exit a competitive industry? One should view rising land values as increasing the **opportunity cost** of one of his inputs.

> *Q: Does the expansion of cities have a different impact on the profitability of large versus small farms? Draw a cost curve that would show how increasing property taxes due to rising land values might affect costs more in smaller firms than in larger ones and justify drawing the curve with that shape. What does this story tell you about how the location of farming will change as cities expand?*

10.14

Downsizing in Major League Baseball—First Time Since 1899? Why? Major League Baseball is really one large business with interrelated plants (each team). In the last ten years, demand by fans, both for tickets to the ballpark and for games on television, has not risen as fast as costs have. When this happens in any other business, the company cuts back production. That's just what may happen in major league ball. And, as in any other business, the plants to be closed are the least productive, the teams that bring in the least **revenue** (sell the fewest seats, have the smallest television audiences) and have been losing money for a long time.

*Q: Draw the **long-run average cost** curves implied by this vignette. Then ask what economic forces caused Major League Baseball to expand from the sixteen teams that existed for most of the first half of the twentieth century. Draw the long-run average cost curves for that change in the market.*

10.15

An article in *The Economist* talks about the "benefits" of recession in that a recession forces companies to try to reduce **total cost.** While competition works, it works slowly, and the fear of going broke, which is more prevalent in a recession, helps competition work faster. Inefficient firms that might survive when times are good are the first ones to close when bad times hit. This is a silver lining in an otherwise dark cloud.

Q: This notion is called the "cleansing effect" of a recession. What are some of the characteristics of companies that are more likely to be cleansed by a recession?

10.16

Last month, Texans voted to impose a limit on cash awards in medical- and product-related tort lawsuits. This change was in reaction to some immense jury awards that had been given for such things as spilled hot coffee at McDonald's. The change was heavily supported by corporations, medical providers, and especially by the insurance industry, which has been complaining about low profits. No doubt this will help insurers' profits in the short run. But once insurance buyers realize that they won't be liable for large awards, the demand for insurance will decrease. In the end, in what is a fairly competitive industry, this decrease in demand will both reduce the cost of insurance and cause the insurance industry to shrink.

Q: The industry will get smaller, but are the little insurance firms or the big ones more likely to survive the downsizing, and why?

10.17

The government of Thailand is trying to regulate its "entertainment" industry, which is notorious throughout Asia for massage parlors, nightclubs, and other venues. It has proposed limiting the hours in which these establishments could be open. The government's proposal is equivalent to a reduction in demand in a **perfectly competitive industry.** No doubt the owners are correct when they argue that the proposals would reduce employment by causing large numbers of establishments to close. Whenever demand drops in such an industry, some incumbents are forced to close, and the equilibrium price of the "commodity" is driven down. The government has responded to the operators' complaints by modifying its proposal, making the restrictions applicable only to new establishments. This amounts to a tax on new establishments—raising their costs relative to incumbents—and is essentially a method of protecting existing firms. It makes entry into the industry more difficult and will reduce the rate at which existing firms that are least efficient are forced to leave the industry. Rather than being a proposal designed to protect consumers (to clean up this industry), the regulations have become a method of aiding operators who were lucky enough to get into the business earlier.

> *Q: What will happen to the price that existing operators will be able to charge for their services?*

10.18

The local camera store and photo-finishing outlet closed, but it had posted a sign urging customers to go to its central location instead. This is a fairly common phenomenon now, as the growth of digital cameras and high-quality color printers has reduced the demand for commercial photo finishing. Grocery stores and drugstores that have photo-finishing sections might be closing them down, too. The question is what this decline in demand will do to the **competitive equilibrium** quantity of camera stores. Will they close, or will the shift help them out compared to nonspecialty stores that have done photo finishing? The eventual location of the most efficient scale of operation in the photography business as a result of the digitization of photography is not clear at this point.

> *Q: How will these changes affect the **long-run average cost** curves facing firms that still do photo finishing? How will they affect the price of this service?*

10.19

Today's *Wall Street Journal* has a story about how the extremely low home mortgage rates have led to huge commissions for mortgage brokers—businesses that help home borrowers find potential lenders. The average broker has doubled his or her earnings compared to five years ago, and owners of brokerage firms have increased their profits even more. Not surprisingly, these huge profits have attracted a tremendous number of smaller new firms into the market. As mortgage rates stop falling, and some of these firms' profits begin to get squeezed, one can expect commissions to become more competitive. The firms will be competing for the increasingly scarce business. At that time, the extraordinary earnings and profits will begin subsiding toward more normal profits—and the least efficient brokerages will be forced to leave the industry.

Q: Do you think that it will be the newer or older firms that survive when demand shifts?

10.20

The first commercial egg bank—which will store unfertilized human ova—will open. Why didn't this industry exist before? Demand and costs. Demand has increased. A growing number of women in their mid-thirties are purposely childless but may want to have a child later on. The technology for operating the bank has been available for a while, but **long-run average cost** has been declining. The conjunction of these two events has given rise to this new industry. Shocks to demand or cost change the equilibrium price, quantity, and number and size of firms in an existing industry, but they also can call into being a new industry— or they can kill off an existing industry (for example, the buggy-whip industry).

Q: List two other completely new industries that have come into existence during your lifetime. List two others that have disappeared during your lifetime.

10.21

The Enron bankruptcy did not mark the end of the energy-trading industry. The product still exists: Enron helped create a market for complex financial products that involve futures prices of various energy commodities. Indeed, with Enron's demise, the survivors in the industry have benefited. My cousin, who runs a small energy-trading business, reports that his company has been doing better than ever since the Enron bankruptcy. This is not surprising: If a competitor disappears from a market and there's no fundamental change in demand in the industry, the surviving firms will profit. The dynamics of competitive industries mean that some firms die while others flourish. The only difficulty for my cousin will come if his profits and those of other survivors attract new competitors. His current success may regrettably be only temporary.

> *Q: What would happen to output and price in the short run, and in the long run, if investors, totally disgusted by the Enron debacle, reduced their willingness to buy the kinds of financial derivatives in which Enron, and my cousin, have specialized?*

CHAPTER 11

Efficiency and Well-Being

11.1

At lunch, a high-paid colleague stood up and said he was going to buy an ice cream. I asked him if he would buy a chocolate-chip cookie for me. He did, and I offered him the dollar it cost when he returned with it. He refused to take my dollar, and I felt very guilty about this. A young colleague, not so well paid, said he would be happy to take my dollar, so I gave it to him. This was clearly **Pareto-improving**: I assuaged my guilt, the young colleague now had a dollar that he did not previously have, and the high-paid colleague must have been at least as well off, or he wouldn't have refused to take my dollar.

> *Q: Is an action Pareto-improving independent of past behavior? If I had known from his past behavior that the high-paid colleague would refuse my dollar, do you think that I would have let him buy me the cookie?*

11.2

This morning, even more deer than usual were grazing on people's lawns and shrubs on my street. (Last Saturday, I saw a ten-point buck in our heavily urbanized area.) Why not allow people to shoot them, thereby increasing the food supply, decreasing the costs of maintaining shrubs and lawns, and providing sport for the residents? The city could even sell hunting licenses and be able to reduce taxes while still balancing its budget. Wouldn't this represent a gain in **efficiency**—cheap venison, too, in the middle of Austin, a city of 750,000 people?

> *Q: Give some reasons why the city might not want to increase economic efficiency in this way, why allowing hunting of urban deer might not be **Pareto-improving**.*

11.3

The chairman of the economics department at another university asked me for a recommendation on a professor they are considering hiring. The professor has lifetime tenure at his current school, but he is not paid very well and not well appreciated by his colleagues. He is occupying a position that has a high **opportunity cost** and that his colleagues would rather fill with someone else. I gave him a very good recommendation—he would fit in better at the new school than in his current job. If he moves, it would be a clear **Pareto improvement:** His current employer would be better off hiring someone else; he would be happier at the new job; and the new school, by the very fact that it is offering him a job, will have demonstrated that it is better off.

> *Q: How might your answer differ for an unmarried professor compared to one with a wife and two children?*

11.4

We were proud sponsors of a concert. When the concert was advertised, we bought two good tickets for it, only to be told that because we had paid to sponsor it, we got two equally good "free tickets." What to do with the extra pair of tickets? We offered the free tickets to various friends, two of whom finally accepted. One friend thanked me profusely. I wanted to tell her that this was a **Pareto-improving** exchange. We get no satisfaction from the extra tickets and are, thus, no worse off if she takes the tickets, but she is better off going to the concert. (She must be; she chose to take the tickets from us.) Indeed, if we feel **altruistic,** we too are better off.

> *Q: If the friend knows that I get pleasure from making her better off, why doesn't she insist that I should also pay her a few dollars? If she did this, compared to a situation in which I don't give her a ticket, would the exchange still represent a Pareto improvement?*

11.5

Before class a student asked, "Can you pass out the problem set assignments far ahead of time? I like to have them before I begin to read the chapters." I asked other students if they wanted them early, and no one said yes. I then asked the other students if they would object to having them way ahead of time. No one objected. Therefore, the only person left in "society" who might be affected by this change is me, the instructor. Since I have the assignments ready two weeks before they are due, it doesn't hurt me to give them out early. The young woman who asked for the problem sets will be helped, and nobody will be hurt if I hand them out early. This is clearly a **Pareto improvement,** so I will start doing it.

> *Q: Suppose I took a vote and a majority, but not all, of the students voted in favor of handing out the problem sets early, but some voted no. Would it represent a Pareto improvement if I went ahead and handed them out?*

11.6

Vignette 5.19 describes the benefits of switching from a system in which each faculty member in a department took as many professional trips as he or she could get the department chair to pay for to a system costing the same in total but with each person limited to a fixed budget of $750. Overall, this made the department chair's life easier, and it also raised the well-being of the average faculty members, since they were now free to spend the money on any kind of professional travel that they felt was valuable. But was this change a **Pareto improvement?** No. Before this change, a few faculty members were taking many trips costing far more in total than $750 per year. Under the new system, those faculty members were restricted to fewer trips than before. They did now have freedom of choice about their travels, but that freedom gave them an outcome that was inferior to what they had before. While society (the department as a whole) was better off, their being worse off ensured that this was not a Pareto improvement.

> *Q: If each faculty member gets $750 per year for travel, can the chair make a Pareto improvement and still cut the total budget for travel?*

11.7

Students' first-draft papers are due in two weeks. I'll mark them, hand them back, and give the students a chance to improve the paper before handing it in for a final grade. One student timidly asks me, "Could I turn mine in a few days early? Would you mind marking it early, so I could have more time for the revision?" I say of course not: My **marginal utility** of grading papers diminishes rapidly with each paper graded in a day, so I'm happy to have her paper alone. Is this a **Pareto improvement?** Yes—the only other people involved are the other students in the class, and there's no reason why our little deal affects their grades or the attention their papers will get. They're no worse off, and she and I are better off.

Q: How would your answer change if I grade on a strict curve, giving a fixed percentage of As, Bs, and so on?

11.8

After using the same textbook for many years, I decided to adopt a different one for next fall's 500-student class. The bookseller was in my office, and she and her boss said I had "made their week." They were really happy about this, since their pay depends in part on what they sell. I was happy, too, as I like the new book and will get pleasure from trying something new. I think my students will be better off, too. This might seem like a **Pareto improvement** because everyone's better off—the students, the bookseller, and me. It isn't: The young woman who sells the book that I had been using is worse off for sure. With fewer of her books sold, her bonus next year will be smaller. Pareto improvements are often difficult to achieve when you consider all the parties that may be involved.

Q: So one person is worse off, but think how many are better off. Isn't that a Pareto improvement? Why, or why not?

11.9

The student newspaper has a story about professor–student sexual relationships. As a free-market economist, I ask: Aren't these relationships **Pareto-improving?** After all, if they are consensual, both parties must be better off. This glib answer is wrong for two reasons. Even if the parties had equal power, third parties are involved: Other students feel slighted when the professor's preferred student is treated differently from them. It's not just envy; it's the possibility that if there is a grading curve or if class time is offered (for example, to present a term paper), the other students suffer. The power is not, however, equal: The student's success in class, in the major, or in a career is controlled or at least influenced by the professor. The power relationship is inherently unequal, so the exchange is inherently not free.

> *Q: How about relationships between professors and former students who are still enrolled? Would they be Pareto-improving? How about relationships between professors and former students who left the university?*

11.10

The state of New York changed its laws regulating the hours in which stores can sell alcohol. Formerly, no sales were allowed on Sundays; now a store can sell on Sunday, provided that it closes on some other day of the week. Only 15 percent of liquor stores have chosen to open on Sunday; those that have report substantial increases in weekly sales: One owner reports, "More sales than Tuesday, half as many hours" (*The New York Times*, February 28, 2004, p. B1). Does this mean that the change in the law has increased New Yorkers' alcohol consumption? Probably not, or not very much; more likely is that there have been small decreases in weekly sales at other stores and on other days of the week when the Sunday-opening stores are open. The **general equilibrium** effects are probably small. But while total boozing hasn't increased much, people are now better off. They can now buy, and perhaps even consume, their liquor at more convenient and desirable times, free of the limits on when they can indulge their desires.

> *Q: The consumer is better off; but might there be others whose position is hurt by this change?*

CHAPTER 12

*M*onopoly and Monopolistic Competition

Monopoly

12.1

Whenever I stay at a hotel, I vow not to buy anything from the minibar. The prices are outrageously high, often twice as much as the same price I would pay at the bar downstairs. Yet occasionally I succumb and buy a beer for $5 or a bottle of water for $3 at 11 PM. Why do the hotels charge so much, given that it surely doesn't cost the hotel that much to stock the drinks in your room? The answer is that they have a **monopoly,** not over the product itself, but over the products at the particular time and place. At 11 PM, having gotten undressed and not wanting to go out again, buying the drink from the minibar is the only way you can satisfy your demand. With demand that locally **inelastic,** the hotel can charge a very high price and still maximize profits. Similar behavior is exhibited by airlines, which are now charging $5 for a beer in coach class. There are no alternatives to buying from the flight attendant if you want a beer during the flight. With demand that inelastic, the price can be jacked up very high.

Q: Why don't airlines allow you to bring beer onto a plane?

12.2

We don't often see the results of a good or service becoming monopolized. Usually we see a monopoly in equilibrium, but rarely a switch to monopoly. The closure of Ansett Airways in Australia has left Qantas Airways with a **monopoly** on a number of major routes, including between Canberra, the capital, and Melbourne, the second-largest city. The results are just what you would expect: There are fewer flights per day, and they are remarkably crowded; and the prices, so people complain, are particularly high on that route. Monopolists do restrict output—and they do charger higher prices than would exist for the same service if there were competition.

Q: Are there airplane routes out of your city that have only one carrier serving them? How do per-mile fares on those routes compare to other routes on which there is competition?

12.3

Until November 2003 in the United States, if you switched cell-phone carriers, your old telephone number died and you had to get a new one. You would face the tremendous hassle of having to tell all your potential callers that your number has changed, so this requirement created a "lock-in effect": It tied users to the cell-phone company they signed up with. It gave your existing cell-phone carrier short-term **monopoly** power over you. Under the Telecommunications Act of 1996, cellular phone carriers are not supposed to do this, but they repeatedly and successfully lobbied the Federal Communications Commission to postpone enforcing that provision of the act. The losers were the consumers—unless they were so smart that they always chose the best firm when they obtained their phones. The winners were the companies that got into the cell-phone business early and locked in customers. Even these quasi-monopolists, however, faced limits: If they raised prices too far above cost, new entrants could attract business by lowering their prices enough to attract customers willing to endure the hassle of getting a new cell-phone number. The administrative changes in November 2003 changed all this, allowing customers to switch carriers without changing their phone numbers. This reduced your existing carrier's monopoly power over you. You still pay a substantial early cancellation penalty if your contract (often two years) with your existing carrier was still in force. That penalty allows your carrier to retain some monopoly power over you.

Q: Try estimating the cost—the hassle—to you of switching the number of your cell phone. Then ask yourself how good a deal a competing company would have to give you on your monthly rate before you would be willing to incur this cost. What are the characteristics of people who are more likely, and less likely, to switch?

12.4

In the last few years, U.S. television shows have been swamped with ads for prescription drugs. Since consumers cannot buy these drugs directly, the ads are intended to induce you to pester your physician to prescribe the drug for you—for things such as anxiety, depression, impotence, and heartburn. One company recently advertised that its new drug is better than the one it has been advertising for many years. Why suddenly campaign against its own drug, and why try to get consumers to ask their doctors to switch? The reason is simple: The patent on the old drug runs out this year, and its price will plummet as other companies are allowed to produce and sell the drug in what will become a highly competitive market. The new ads are a way of building loyalty to a new, monopolized brand at a time when the old **monopoly** will disappear.

> *Q: Microsoft introduces new operating systems for personal computers every three or four years. How is that behavior similar to or different from the introduction of the new drug described here?*

12.5

A *Wall Street Journal* story talks about universities and colleges building cemeteries and mausoleums on campus and selling burial space to alumni. Each university is a **monopolist** in this (no University of Texas alum would wish to be buried on any other campus). The question is what price to charge for the plots. Some of the institutions in the story must be charging too much—they built a huge number of plots, and almost none have been sold. Others have excess demand—nearly all the available plots were snapped up at the initial offering. Their price is clearly too low. To find the price for the existing plots, the schools need to think about what their demand curve looks like and set the price to equate demand and the existing fixed supply. To find the right number of plots to build, like any other monopolist, the schools need to discover what the demand curve is and build enough so that **marginal revenue** equals the **marginal cost.** (This must include the **opportunity cost** of the university's space. Remember, the land and space could be built up with classrooms, dorms, a student union, or even left as a greenbelt or park on campus.)

> Q: *Are there other institutions that might consider putting cemeteries next to their buildings? How should they price the burial plots?*

12.6

A recent television ad for Depends, the protective underwear for senior citizens, asked, "How to improve the protection of Depends? Lower the price!" Presumably, the ad means that people can now buy more of the product and, thus, get more protection. This is true as long as Depends does not have a completely **inelastic demand.** But even if the demand were somewhat inelastic, the company would not lower its price, as **revenue** would drop while the **total cost** of production would rise. It must be the case that the manufacturer believes that it has a highly **elastic demand** (appropriately enough for underwear). Its managers must think that the price cut will generate such a large increase in quantity sold that revenue will rise more than enough to offset the increase in total cost. A more accurate ad, thus, would ask, "How to improve the protection of Depends *a lot?* Lower the price!"

> Q: *Even before any extra Depends are sold, the new advertising campaign costs the company money. How does this cost affect the* **price elasticity of demand** *that is required before it will pay the company to lower the price?*

12.7

It's tough to be a **monopolist.** Witness the continuing efforts of the diamond **monopoly**—De Beers Consolidated and its Central Selling Organization—to make sure that people continue buying diamond jewelry and do not sell the diamond jewelry they already own. De Beers has a new TV ad for a "three-diamond" ring and even has a new piece of music to replace the pseudo-baroque theme it has been using for at least ten years. These endeavors follow its efforts to lure more established families into buying a second diamond (a twenty-fifth wedding anniversary token of love) and its successful expansion of the diamond ring as a wedding token to newly affluent Asian countries. De Beers's main problem is not so much its potential competitors, although new diamond discoveries outside its control do pose continual concerns. Instead, it is the need, faced by every monopolist, to make sure that the **demand curve** is pushed out as far as it can be.

> *Q: Would you buy your fiancée (or let your fiancé buy you) a turquoise engagement ring? What would happen to De Beers, which would remain the diamond monopolist, if people began accepting turquoise as a substitute for diamonds?*

12.8

Justice William Brennan served on the U.S. Supreme Court for thirty-four years. As he neared retirement in the late 1980s, he put severe restrictions on access to his papers, allowing only one lawyer/journalist access to most of the material. The material was to be opened to everyone only in 2017. There was to be no competition among potential biographers to write the definitive work about this important jurist. A **monopoly** was granted to one person, just as the government grants a patent to a company for some invention. Not surprisingly, given the lack of competition, as of 2004 the potential biographer still had not published the biography; and in interviews he admits he has written only one-third of a book, the same amount he acknowledged having completed in 1997. No doubt shortly before 2017, as the possibility of competition becomes imminent, the monopoly biographer will race to complete his book, lest others use their access to "scoop" him.

> *Q: Governments in most countries keep official documents secret for fixed periods of time after they are written. What do you think happens to the number of books published about a particular time period in the few years after the restriction on documents ends?*

12.9

The old James Bond movie *Live and Let Die* begins with a funeral procession in New Orleans. In the movie, Mr. Big, the chief villain, hatches a scheme to give heroin away—free—in the United States. The purpose of this plan is to drive out his competitors. Once he has succeeded in monopolizing the market, he plans to raise prices to their **monopoly** level. He implicitly believes that the short-run losses he incurs by giving the drug away will be more than made up for by the monopoly profits he will make once his competitors have been driven out of the market. His predatory pricing—selling below **average variable cost**—makes sense only if he can survive those losses better than his competitors can, and if he believes it will be difficult for new competitors to come into the market. If he's correct, he will reap monopoly profits for a long time.

> *Q: Will Mr. Big's plan work better if the demand for heroin is inelastic or if it's elastic?*

12.10

One night, a student was driving from Austin to Houston, as she often does. As she approached a Houston suburb, she noticed a strange sight. On the right was an H.E.B. store, a major Texas supermarket chain, that also had gasoline pumps in its parking area. On the left was an independent gas station. On her previous drives, all of which had been during the daytime when the H.E.B. was open, prices at the two outlets were identical. At night, with the H.E.B. closed, the independent station was posting a price that was 2 cents above the price that both it and the H.E.B. charged when the H.E.B. was open. Without the competition, the little local **monopoly** was now able to raise the price.

> *Q: Look for similar behavior in your town, for example, different pricing by convenience stores late at night compared to daytime.*

12.11

Whenever the cost of a first-class stamp is raised, the U.S. Postal Service (USPS) undertakes a new advertising campaign. I doubt that advertising will help much, at least not in the part of its business involving letters and bills. The problem is that the long-run cost of transmitting paper documents is rising, while the long-run cost of transmitting electrons (fax, e-mails, electronic funds transfers) is falling. The cost of a one-minute fax has fallen below 10 cents at the same time that stamp prices have risen. Until the 1980s, we mailed checks every month for the phone, electricity, gas, and mortgage. We now have these all directly debited; it's easier, and the companies save money this way, too. The only hope for the USPS in the long run is in its lines of business where goods must be sent: parcels and express mail. Whether it is efficient enough to compete in these areas with FedEx, UPS, DHL, and others is another question.

*Q: The USPS has a **monopoly** on sending letters. Why doesn't that monopoly guarantee it **economic profits** forever?*

12.12

Two of my economics major students were commenting on how good the food is at the privately run food stand on campus and how they hoped that the young immigrant who runs it makes lots of money. I hope not, and I bet not. The university leases the rights to set up a stand in that location. The university has a **monopoly** on the space on campus, while the number of potential bidders to operate food stands is large. If the officials who determine which stands can be operated are clever, they should extract from the winning bidder all profits above what he or she would earn in a competitive market. The winner would make just enough to cover capital costs and the **opportunity cost** of labor time. If the university does not receive this much from the lease it writes, then it will be sharing its monopoly profits with the operator of the food stand. It will be reducing the university's **revenue** and hurting the citizens, who pay taxes to the state that supports the university, and the students who pay tuition.

*Q: Are there any reasons why the university might not want to push the winning bidder down to zero **economic profits?***

12.13

Between 2000 and 2001, the average price of a ticket to a rock concert rose much more rapidly than did the rate of inflation. At the same time, total rock ticket **revenue** fell. It's possible that the **monopoly** promoters of rock concerts raised prices to the point where they had an **elastic demand,** so they lost more revenue from audience members who stayed away from concerts than they gained from the higher prices paid by audiences that continued attending. Alternatively, perhaps the mild economic recession of 2001 reduced the demand for rock concerts generally.

With just this information, it's hard to tell whether the monopoly promoters followed the correct pricing strategy.

*Q: If you were a monopoly seller of rock concert tickets and believed that the decline in revenue had occurred because you had moved onto the elastic part of your **demand curve**, what would you do with the ticket price? If you believed it was caused by the recession, what would you do with the ticket price?*

12.14

Counterfeit Pigs. The *Wall Street Journal* reports about the problems of the manufacturers of Parma hams. Parma, Italy, prides itself on being the ham capital of the world. Hams labeled Parma sell for very high prices, and that's the problem: Producers of other hams sell hams with the Parma label at lower prices, shifting demand away from the true Parma product. The Parma ham producers' cooperative uses a variety of labeling practices and even has ham inspectors across the European Union. This helps restrict competition, but it doesn't solve the problem of competition from falsely labeled products sold outside the EU. As always with a **monopoly,** competitors try to compete away some of the monopoly profits, and the monopolist has to expend resources trying to stamp out the competition.

Q: Public schools are often monopoly suppliers of K–12 education. What competition do they face, and how do they try to reduce it?

Monopolistic Competition

12.15

The *Wall Street Journal* reports on a "problem" facing a number of famous northeastern prep schools. Less wealthy schools that play in the same basketball league have been recruiting potential basketball stars and destroying teams from Exeter, Phillips, Choate, and their peers. The administrators at these schools don't like the embarrassment of fifty-point losses and have proposed the creation of a new league that would exclude the upstarts. In essence, they wish to banish competition by offering a differentiated product—a well-financed education with implicit limits on basketball prowess—from what the less famous schools offer. This is standard economic behavior: If you are losing out in a market, use **product differentiation** and try to exclude the "firms" that previously had a competitive advantage.

Q: Suppose you were the athletic director at one of these elite schools. Provide arguments in favor of banning the upstarts from your league that might appear less narrow-minded.

12.16

The market for apartment rentals around campus is certainly not characterized by a **monopoly**—there are lots of sellers. But it's not **perfectly competitive** either, as there is **product differentiation** among apartments by location, amenities (age, Internet access, etc.) and no doubt other factors. The market is best characterized as **monopolistic competition.** What happens in this kind of market when the demand curve in the entire market shifts to the left, as it does every summer when the student population decreases compared to the regular academic year? The market responds just as our theory predicts—the prices asked for the same apartment appear to be about one-third lower than they are during the regular semesters. I would bet, too, that there are more vacancies in the summer than during the academic year—the equilibrium quantity is lower.

Q: What other monopolistically competitive industries around campus suffer the same seasonal declines in price and industry output?

12.17

Your main text is one of around thirty economics principles books. These books appear in new editions every two or three years. Why? Partly because the material becomes obsolete fairly quickly. But if that were the sole cause, we wouldn't also see new editions of basic math books every few years: It's hard to believe that college math changes every three years. Frequent new editions also can't stem from the used-book market killing off sales of new copies: If that were true, the book publishers would price high enough to account for the multiple resales of each new copy. Anyway, in economics the three-year cycle started before there was much of a used-book market. The best explanation is a combination of the partial obsolescence of the material and the need for the **monopolistic competitors** to **differentiate the product** from its competitors by adding new bells and whistles in new editions. Each book tries to carve out a niche in the market in terms of difficulty of presentation and style of approach. When another book in that niche adds a new feature—online updates, interactive CD-ROMs, or whatever—its competitors must update their editions to remain viable. If there were no obsolescence of the material, new editions might not come so frequently. But the books would still be revised regularly as a competitive response to the revisions of the slightly differentiated products with which they compete.

> *Q: The decision to assign the texts is made by your professor. If students could choose the book, would they choose an old edition or a new edition? Why? Would the cycle of new editions be as rapid as it now is?*

12.18

A local grocery store has a truly immense array of famous brands of beer from all over the world, with lots of examples of micro-brews from all regions of the United States. How can a small brand stand out from the shelves against all this competition? In other words, how can the manufacturer practice **product differentiation** and get the customer's attention? These companies have no national advertising budgets; they are not sponsoring the Super Bowl. The trick appears to be some clever eye-catching name. Years ago we saw Black Dog and Pete's Wicked Ale. Today we have Arrogant Bastard Ale, a fairly heavy brew whose label tells the customer that he or she probably isn't tough enough to drink this bottle and should instead buy one of the wimpy standard brands with a multi-million-dollar advertising budget. That is a clever name and a clever challenge. While I didn't buy a bottle, it has stuck in my mind and probably will win me over the next time I shop.

> *Q: Think up a name for a brand of beer that you will create. The only requirements are that your brand name cannot be unprint-able in a family newspaper (not a very stringent standard today) and must be the best possible name to sell more of the beer.*

CHAPTER 13

Price Discrimination

13.1

Disney World offers tourists a three-day pass that costs several hundred dollars. But Floridians can obtain the same pass for a bit more than $100. This is a great example of demand-based **price discrimination.** The cost to Disney of letting a Floridian or an out-of-stater into the park is the same. But the out-of-staters, having traveled to Florida, often with the sole purpose of visiting Disney World, have a very inelastic demand, while the Floridians have lots of other ways they can spend time while at home. Their demand is more **elastic.** It is easy for Disney to separate the two markets. All it needs to do is to ask those people seeking to purchase the cheap tickets to show a Florida driver's license.

> *Q: Is there any way you can get around Disney's clever way of separating the markets for these discount passes?*

13.2

While visiting a Dutch university a few years ago, I wanted to buy a cup of coffee. The choice was the cafeteria or a vending machine in the same building. The cafeteria was open, so I bought my cup there. At 7 PM, I went back to buy another cup. The cafeteria was closed, so I went to the vending machine. The price for a cup of coffee was higher than it had been during the day; the vending machine was programmed to require a higher price at times when there was no competition from the cafeteria. The cost of restocking and servicing the coffee machine doesn't depend on when the vending machine coffee was consumed. The vending machine company price discriminates by charging a lot when the substitute—the cafeteria—isn't available, when there is an **inelastic demand** for the vending machine's coffee. It prices lower when the cafeteria is open—when demand is more **elastic**.

> *Q: How would you behave if your dormitory installed variable-price vending machines near the cafeteria and charged higher prices on food when the cafeteria is closed?*

13.3

A bottle of eighteen-year-old single-malt Scotch whiskey typically is priced at least twice that of the same distillery's twelve-year-old product. Why is the eighteen-year-old malt so much more expensive? After all, the production cost to the distiller is less than 50 percent more than the younger malt. The only extra cost is the additional six years of aging in the cask. The reason must be that the distillers recognize that only real Scotch drinkers are going to buy the more mature whiskey. They assume that such aficionados have a lower **price elasticity of demand** for Scotch than does the average whiskey drinker. They **price discriminate** based on their ability to separate the markets for the different types of Scotch (the consumer who buys the less expensive, younger whiskey can't convert it into the more desirable product) and the different demand elasticities of the two types of buyers.

> *Q: How does your answer change if people get pleasure from snobbishly showing that they are willing to serve the more expensive Scotch to their guests?*

13.4

As you approach Los Angeles International Airport by car, the price of regular gasoline changes dramatically. The stations near the freeway exit charge about 30 cents a gallon less than does the last gas station before the car rental return offices. If you go farther beyond the airport, prices again drop off quickly. The stations are **price discriminating** to take advantage of the customers' different **price elasticities of demand**. Customers who have waited until just before the rental office face the choice of gassing up for $2.35 or of letting the rental company charge them over $5 per gallon to fill up. The station's only competition is the rental company; and the $5 price limits what the nearby station can charge. Markets are neatly separated—you won't drive back to a cheaper station once you're near the rental office, and you can't buy gasoline from some sidewalk peddler who has gotten it cheaper.

Q: If this is true, why doesn't the gas station nearest the car rental offices charge $5 per gallon?

13.5

There are many cases where new customers get a better deal than old customers do. This is true for sales from the Victoria's Secret catalog: The company's computerized records tell it when you last bought. The catalog offers lower prices if your last purchase was a long time ago. Similarly, this week RoadRunner cable modems are offering a $19.95 monthly price for three months (instead of the usual $44.95) if you sign on now. Both represent good examples of pure demand-based **price discrimination:** The good or service offered is identical, and the only difference between customers is how wedded to the good or service they appear to be. The companies assume that frequent buyers or long-term users will buy anyway and, thus, they have an **inelastic demand.** Another precondition for price discrimination is met, too: The companies are sure beforehand that the low-priced good or service—the lingerie or the high-speed Internet connection—will not be resold.

Q: We don't see this kind of pricing behavior by auto retailers. Why not?

13.6

I sit down in a fancy restaurant in Denmark and see that there is a fixed-price menu. Appetizers, first courses, main courses, cheese course, and dessert course are possible. You can get two courses for 295 Danish kronor (DKK, about $50), three for DKK330, four for DKK385, or five for DKK445. The marginal price of an extra course is, thus, DKK35 for the third course, DKK45 for the fourth course, and DKK60 for the fifth course. Surely, everybody's first two courses will include the main course and one from among the appetizer, cheese course, or dessert course. Thus, it makes sense that the average price for two courses is much more than the average price of four courses, since the main course is the most costly to prepare. But why is the marginal price that I must pay for extra courses increasing? The answer may be demand-based **price discrimination.** Perhaps those customers who are willing to pay for a fourth or fifth course are those who are real gourmets (or simply like to "pig out"), so that their **demand elasticity** is less than that of other people. Charging more for these subsequent courses is a way the restaurant can exploit their lower demand elasticity.

Q: Is this kind of pricing more or less likely in a big city, with lots of fancy restaurants, or in a smaller city that has very few gourmet restaurants?

13.7

We spent Labor Day weekend at my aunt's funeral in Los Angeles. She is "buried" in an outdoor, above-ground crypt, essentially a ten-foot-high ten-foot-thick wall that contains a large number of columns, each with seven niches piled on top of each other. Each niche contains two caskets. The owners of the crypt charge different prices depending on where in the column the niche is located. The highest prices are for niches 3, 4, and 5—the ones that are roughly eye-level—while the lowest prices are for the top and bottom niches. The differences in price can't be based on costs— indeed, the **marginal cost** of building the top niche is probably higher than that of the middle niches. The price differences must be due to demand-based **price discrimination.** People want to be able to see their loved one's grave at eye level and do not want to need to bend over or stand on a ladder to touch it or view it closely.

Q: The crypts are bought in most cases before the person is dead, with the person himself or herself often deciding which niche to purchase. Why might the person care which one is bought?

13.8

Maybe it makes sense to look into buying higher-octane gas instead of regular 87-octane gas. The prices of 89-octane and 93-octane gas are 14 cents and 20 cents above that of the 87-octane gas at my local station, differences that seem typical of those around town. Does this difference reflect cost-based **price discrimination?** Or is it demand-based price discrimination? Experts on the industry tell me that the difference in the **marginal cost** of production between 87- and 93-octane gas is about 5 cents. Most of the price difference is due to demand-based price discrimination. My car takes any kind of gasoline, so I can choose which type to buy. But some car owners are locked into the higher-octane gasoline: Their demand is necessarily less elastic, as they do not have a choice about whether to buy low-octane gas. Still, other drivers mistakenly think that their autos, which will run perfectly well on low-octane gas, will run better with higher-octane gas. They have an **inelastic demand** because of their incorrect beliefs.

> *Q: What would be the effect on the price differences for the different octane gasolines if a consumer group launched a publicity campaign demonstrating that most cars run just as well on lower-octane gas?*

13.9

A student has a job as a hunting guide on a game ranch in the Texas Hill Country. He reports that the ranch charges $1,000 for the right to shoot a "trophy" deer, but only $500 for the right to shoot a deer in a cull—to help thin the herd. The difference between the kinds of deer has to do with the size of their antlers—the number of prongs and the spread between them, with a particular score indicating the cutoff between the two types of deer. The ranch **price discriminates.** It relies on the likelihood that the hunters' demand for trophy deer is less elastic than for cull deer and sets prices accordingly. Its problem is trying to keep the two markets separate. The hunters want the best looking deer for their wall, but they do respond to price. A cull deer whose antlers are just below the cutoff on size is almost as good as one whose antlers are just big enough. Not surprisingly, hunters make a special point of trying to shoot the largest of the deer that still qualify for the cut-rate price on cull deer.

> *Q: How would the ranch's pricing policy be affected if better rifle scopes become available to hunters?*

13.10

Resident undergrads at the University of Texas at Austin pay $6,500 a year for tuition; nonresidents pay over twice as much. Why does the university **price discriminate,** since the **marginal cost** of educating in-state and out-of-state students is about the same? One rationale is **equity:** Parents of in-state students pay the taxes that cover about 20 percent of the university's costs. But out-of-state tuition seems too high to be justified on this basis alone. Instead, it's a way that the state raises **revenue**—it represents demand-based price discrimination. The university is not a **monopoly,** but it does have some monopoly power. Out-of-state students who are especially interested in the fun of being in Austin, Texas, or who want a particular major that the university is very good in (petroleum engineering, for example) are willing to pay the high tuition. A very large fraction of out-of-state students say that there is something very special about the university that attracted them (and that made them willing to pay this high tuition).

> *Q: What does this discussion suggest will be true about the mix of in-state and out-of-state hotel majors at Michigan State University, one of the few institutions to offer a hotel management major?*

13.11

A student mentioned the small seasonal business he runs. He picks up your used Christmas tree, throws it into his pickup truck, and disposes of it for you. The Christmas trees differ little in size, but he charges a higher price if the distance from the house to the street is longer so that he has to work harder. This is surely cost-based **price discrimination.** He also mentioned, though, that he once charged a higher price to a woman in curlers and slippers. He figured that she was much less willing to drag the tree by herself than were most of his customers. Believing she had an **inelastic demand,** he quoted her a higher price than usual. This probably would be illegal or at least severely frowned upon for a larger business, but it is a good example of demand-based price discrimination.

> *Q: If he believed she had an inelastic demand, why didn't he charge her $500 for the service? What does your answer say about how the* **price elasticity of demand** *changes as the price of the service changes?*

13.12

Verdi's opera *Rigoletto* includes a character who is a professional assassin. He tells the court jester Rigoletto, who would like to have the Duke, his employer, assassinated, "[I'm] an expert swordsman . . . a man who'll rid you of a rival for a pittance." Rigoletto asks, "For a nobleman, how much would you require?" The assassin answers, "That would be somewhat higher." Why does the assassin charge more for killing a nobleman? Is it cost-based **price discrimination?** Is killing a nobleman riskier in the sense that the likelihood of being killed or caught is greater? Or is it pure price discrimination because a client who wants to have a nobleman killed has a lower **price elasticity of demand** and is, thus, willing to pay more than a client who wants a commoner assassinated? Both possibilities are consistent with behavior in the opera.

> *Q: How would you answer this question if you knew for sure that the assassin would be leaving town immediately after the deed and would never be caught?*

CHAPTER 14

*O*ligopoly (Including Game Theory)

Games

14.1

Strategic Behavior on an Airplane (best understood if you draw the seat configuration of the airplane). I was sitting on an airplane going from Frankfurt, Germany, to Dallas. In the three-seat row in front of me, the middle seat was empty. In the three-seat row in front of that, both the middle and right-hand seats were empty. The guy in the left seat one row ahead of me moved to the center seat. The man in the right seat of that row was thus crowded, got annoyed, and moved one row forward. The piggish man then lay down and stretched out, as he now had the whole row to himself. His strategy could have failed—he might have had to spend some time in the center seat next to the other guy if the other fellow hadn't moved. But the other fellow did move, so his strategy was successful.

> *Q: Say you were the man in the right seat of the row ahead of me and you were unwilling to move and didn't like to be pushed around or liked teaching piggish people a lesson. What behavior would you have engaged in to induce the piggish man to retreat to his original seat?*

14.2

A student described a problem he had with his younger brother. His mom always insisted they clean up their room while she was away; and he knew that Mom would blame him, not the younger brother, if the task weren't done. This is a classic game-theory problem. The two parties are you and your little brother; the strategies are Work and Loaf; and the **"payoff bimatrix"** is

		Little Bro	
		Work	Loaf
	Work	(3,1)	(2,4)
You			
	Loaf	(4,1)	(1,4)

Work and Loaf are each of your strategies, and the pair (3,1) indicates that your payoff is 3, his is 1, if you both work. The other pairs are read similarly. Now it's not clear what you should do—you're not uniformly better off independent of what he does. But it is clear for him: No matter what you do, he's better off loafing. Loafing for him is a **dominant strategy.** You know that; therefore, you choose to Work, because you're better off working if he Loafs than loafing if he Loafs. (If you both Loaf, your mom punishes you and not him.)

> *Q:* *How would the payoff bimatrix change if your Mom were to punish both of you equally if the task were not done?*

14.3

One of the well-known game-theory examples is called the Battle of the Sexes game. This came to life for me one spring weekend in 1994. The movie *Little Women* had opened, and my wife desperately wanted to see it. The thought turned my stomach, especially because another, locally made movie about young women, *Teenage Catgirls in Heat,* was playing in town. My wife had no interest in seeing that. The alternative to going out was staying home and watching a *Star Trek* rerun. We would have been together watching the rerun, which was better than being separated and watching separate movies, but we wouldn't have been very happy. There is no single solution to this game, so I proposed that we alternate by seeing *Little Women* that weekend and *Catgirls* the next. This "mixed-strategy" idea is an equilibrium solution for this game. We saw *Little Women,* and my wife was happy. Regrettably,

Catgirls never showed after that weekend. Years later, I bought a DVD of it and, sadly, wasted 90 minutes watching what was a truly awful movie.

Q: What would the outcome have been if either my wife or I had preferred to see the other person's movie rather than watch the Star Trek *rerun?*

14.4

We have lots of outside speakers who visit the Economics Department and present one-and-a-half-hour seminars in which they lecture about their current research. Some seminars are expected to be excellent, while a few others are unlikely to interest more than three faculty members. To have only three faculty members show up at a seminar is an embarrassment for the department. The chair has begun to have the department's administrative assistant go around to faculty offices before the seminars he expects to be poorly attended and ask the faculty members to attend. This approach may work for a while, but once faculty members get used to it and learn to predict which seminars will generate this sort of cajoling, they will be sure to be out of their offices before the probably poorly attended seminars. The **Nash equilibrium** here is poor attendance, with most faculty members making sure to hide out to avoid the chair or his agents.

*Q: How is this game similar to the standard **prisoners' dilemma** problem in game theory? Help the chair out by suggesting things that he can do to get the "society" (the Department of Economics) out of what appears to be a Nash equilibrium that is like a prisoners' dilemma.*

14.5

Another professor has caught a cheater. It's an open and shut case. If the professor files a formal charge with the university, however, she may be required to participate in a long judicial hearing. Her strategies are File the Charge and Don't File. If she does file the charge, the student faces universitywide disciplinary charges. The professor has given the student the choice of taking a course grade one level below what he otherwise would receive or facing a university hearing that could lead to his expulsion. Which choice—which strategy—will the student pick? Unless the student is a tremendous risk lover, he will choose to take the lower course grade and not risk expulsion. Taking the lower grade is his **dominant strategy.** The professor knew this when structuring the choices for the cheater, and she designed the choices to minimize the time she would have to spend on this case.

> *Q: Is this equilibrium **Pareto-optimal;** that is, are both parties at least as well off as they would be in any other outcome of these strategies?*

14.6

A large number of Ph.D. students who are seeking faculty jobs have their own Web sites. Many of the people from one particular university have posted their pictures. The first three women are extraordinarily good-looking, and the first two men are remarkably handsome. I begin to think, "In addition to producing good students, this economics department also produces good-looking students." The next student, however, has no picture, and the same is true for three of the eight others. I then think that perhaps only those students who are good-looking post their pictures on the Web. But even if those without pictures were good-looking, I would infer they are ugly, since they failed to put their pictures up. If pictures are allowed and those I see are handsome or beautiful, I will always infer that those who are left out are ugly. As long as you believe that those people who don't have pictures up are on average worse-looking than you, it pays to put your own picture on your Web site. Once the best-looking post their pictures, it pays the next-best-looking to post his or hers, and so on. The **Nash equilibrium** of this game has everyone except the ugliest person posting his or her picture.

> *Q: Does the same behavior carry over into résumés used by college students looking for jobs when they graduate? Would you put your picture on your résumé? Why, or why not? Would it be better if universities forbade students from posting pictures on their Web sites or résumés?*

14.7

At the end of our annual beach week, our sons and their wives need to pack up. My highest **marginal product** at that time is entertaining the grandchildren and getting them out of the way. I suggested to the kids that I take them to the beach one last time, but they said they wanted to stay home. Both they and I know we have to stay together. In descending order of desirability, my preferences are beach with them, stay home with them, beach without them, home without them (which is not likely). Their preferences are stay home with me, go to the beach with me, stay home without me, go to the beach without me. There is no **Nash equilibrium** in this game, which is a classic Battle of the Sexes game. If we had several days, we could follow a mixed-strategy equilibrium—go to the beach together one morning, stay home the next, and so on. But we don't—we have just this final morning. The solution for me is simple: Don't let this become a game, and use a **first-mover advantage** by saying to the kids: "I'm going to the beach—do you want to come?" Having said that they, of course, preferred going to the beach with me rather than staying home by themselves, so off we went to the beach!

Q: If you were one of the grandchildren, what could you have done to get the outcome you desired?

14.8

I've built up a reputation for being completely, perhaps even brutally, honest in my recommendations for students and evaluations of people for jobs and promotion. Being honest in these matters is an investment in reputation: If you're honest for a while, people will believe you thereafter. The problem is that incentives may change in the final years of a career. Why maintain a strategy of honesty when there is no future reputation to be affected? Why not be increasingly overoptimistic about students' likely future success, since by the time I'm proved wrong I won't be writing any more letters? The problem with this thinking is that the people reading the letters may be equally aware that the end is in sight for me. They will deduce my incentives to shade the letters toward excessive optimism and will pay them appropriately little attention. Knowing that, I had better remain honest. The only way out, if I want to play this finite game, is to write glowing recommendations, make people uncertain about the end of my career, and surprise people by suddenly retiring and ceasing to write recommendations.

Q: What does this vignette tell you about which professors you should approach for recommendations for internships, jobs, and graduate school?

14.9

In *American Pie 2,* a guy tells his buddy that with women you need to use the Rule of Three: To find the truth, multiply by three the number of guys a woman says she's slept with. In the next scene, a woman tells her friend that with guys you need to use the Rule of Three: To find the truth, divide by three the number of women a guy says he's slept with. Assume that each sex believes its own Rule of Three about the other sex, that guys seek to impress women with their prowess, and that women seek to impress guys with their demureness. What will each sex's strategy be, and what will the equilibrium be? Guys will claim as many women as is remotely credible; if they know women will divide by three, they should multiply the actual number by four. Women will claim as much demureness as is remotely credible; if they know guys will multiply by three, they should divide the actual number by four. The equilibrium will not be the truth or even three times (for men) and one-third (for women) of the truth. Instead, the sexes will go to opposite extremes, restrained only by the credibility of their claims. Rules of Three may be only a temporary equilibrium: If both sexes realize what's going on, each may develop a Rule of Four, a Rule of Five, or more.

> *Q: What if a woman announces that she is telling the truth? How will guys' strategies change?*

14.10

The novel *Thinks . . .* by David Lodge (New York: Viking, 2001) ends with the main character, a noted adulterer, discovering that his wife is having an affair. He remarks, "It was tit for tat. She had defected knowing that he had defected." The author clearly views marriage as a repeated **prisoners' dilemma,** one in which each spouse has the strategies Cheat, Don't Cheat. He implies that the desirable equilibrium is each party choosing Don't Cheat. The protagonist's wife, trying to punish him, has chosen the strategy Cheat in the hopes of getting her husband back to the desired equilibrium. Punishment in a repeated prisoners' dilemma is a good strategy: If my rival cuts price below cost, I can do the same thing, but for a while this strategy hurts both of us. Worse still, in a marriage each party has the option of not staying around to bear the punishment: Each could file for divorce and end this most dangerous game.

> *Q: Would you be more or less careful to make sure that your spouse doesn't find out that you are cheating if divorce is a possibility?*

14.11

During the beach week with the children and grandchildren, the grandkids decided that my name is "Tammy," and they called me that the entire week. On the last day, the four-year-old asked, "Grandpa Dan, if you give me a dollar I won't call you Tammy any more." I thought this was a good deal and gave a dollar to her, her brother, and her cousins, all of whom made the same promise. Was this a good strategy on my part—was my behavior **subgame perfect** in the context of the **repeated game** that is our beach week each summer? *No*—my behavior was not subgame perfect. They will probably not call me Tammy again. (I told them that if they did, they would have to pay me one dollar *plus interest.*) But next summer they could, for example, start calling me Georgina or something equally silly for a fifty-nine-year-old man. If I played the same strategy next summer, the grandkids could wind up taking me for a dollar per grandkid each summer. If they pick a name next summer, you can be sure that I will not choose the subgame imperfect strategy of paying them not to call me that *particular* name! In fact, my surmise about their behavior was correct: I saw all four kids just three months later at a family occasion—and they all immediately decided that my name was "Cheesie," and called me that the entire time! This time, though, I didn't try to buy them off.

> *Q: What should I have told them about names for me when I paid the four grandkids a dollar each?*

14.12

When my sons were eleven and eight, they developed the very annoying habit of calling each other obscene names based on body parts below the waist. The name-calling often resulted in physical fights. Faced with this, my wife and I decided to stop it by saying, "No more names below the waist!" Whoever used such names would be sent to his room for the rest of the day. The next day, which was the next round of the **repeated game** involving the kids and us, the older boy came to breakfast and snarled at the younger boy, "You're an elbow!" The younger boy got angry, yelled, "You're a shoulder!" and they started fighting. Our strategy of outlawing "names below the waist" was not **subgame perfect**—it failed to get them to alter their behavior. They quickly adapted to our restriction and continued fighting. After a few days we adopted the strategy of telling them that *any* name-calling would result in isolation. That strategy was subgame perfect; the name-calling stopped.

> *Q: Who are the players in the game? What if the boys, instead of fighting, colluded against us; what could they have done—what would you have done?*

Oligopoly Behavior and Antitrust Policy

14.13

Digital TV is much better than analog—a crisper picture, better sound, and less space required on the radio spectrum to send the signal. For at least five years, TV manufacturers have been able to make and install digital tuners; and for at least that long, broadcasters have been able to send digital signals. Yet only a tiny fraction of TVs and TV broadcasting is digital. This is a **prisoner's dilemma:** Manufacturers must choose between Make Digital, Don't Make Digital. Make Digital is profitable only if there are lots of digital broadcasts. Broadcasters must choose between Broadcast Digital, Don't Broadcast Digital. Broadcasting Digital is profitable only if there are lots of digital TVs. The **equilibrium** is Don't Make, Don't Broadcast. Everyone is worse off—this is an inferior equilibrium, but neither side wants to risk the chance that the other side won't go digital. The government is imposing a solution: TVs must have digital tuners by 2007. The new equilibrium will be Make Digital, Broadcast Digital. Both manufacturers and broadcasters will be better off, since the more attractive viewing will bring in more customers. But without intervention from outside this game, the desirable equilibrium would not be reached.

> *Q: Write down a **payoff bimatrix** for this game, and show that the initial equilibrium is Don't/Don't.*

14.14

Textbook publishers customarily send professors free "examination copies" of books they would like the professors to require their students to buy. A game theorist colleague received an advertisement for a textbook on game theory. The publisher will send an examination copy if the professor returns a reply post-card and $3. Why the $3 charge? It's a trivial amount, not even enough to cover the **marginal cost** of printing and sending the book. The strategy is presumably designed to avoid sending books to professors who have no intention of assigning them in class. The publisher defected from the **Nash equilibrium** of free copies for interested professors. My colleague has three strategies: forget it, instead send in the $3 with the postcard, or a third, clever strategy—send in the postcard with no money and punish the defector. He chose the third strategy. My guess is that other good game theorists will, too. They will call the publisher's bluff. I expect the publisher will find that adding this charge doesn't work, and the game will revert to the Nash equilibrium of free copies to any interested professor.

> **Q:**   *How would my colleague's strategy change if the charge had been $10? Would a different charge alter the Nash equilibrium?*

14.15

The Antitrust Division of the U.S. Department of Justice must approve mergers between American companies. It charges companies a fee of $75,000 to review a medium-sized merger and $150,000 to review a larger merger. The division can be viewed as the **monopoly** seller of "merger approvals," and the companies that are merging can be viewed as the **monopsony** buyers of approvals from the division. A buyer will presumably gain additional profits when the merger is approved. Otherwise, why seek the merger? This situation is a **bilateral monopoly**—one buyer, one seller—in which there is some pot of extra profit that will be generated after the merger. The question is: Why does the division charge so little? Surely the merger is worth far more to the parties than the measly $75,000, or even $150,000, that the division charges. The $75,000 far exceeds the cost of the division's workers' time and, in fact, in a good year the division returns over $200 million to the U.S. Treasury. If it were a profit-maximizer, it would charge a lot more—it would bargain for a large chunk of the profits to be generated by the merger. It doesn't maximize profits, though—political pressures limit its ability to extract much of the merger's profits and return them to the taxpayer.

> **Q:**   *If this were a competitive industry and the merger generated gains in efficiency in production, who would benefit from the merger, and why? Since it is a monopoly, who benefits, and why?*

14.16

Our clothes dryer died yesterday, so we went out shopping for a new one. I said we should go to Sears, but my wife thought that Sears carries only its own brand (Kenmore) of appliances. I thought that that was no longer true, and I was correct: A few years ago, Sears began carrying all major brands and trying to compete with the discount appliance stores. Why did Sears switch strategies after so many years of advertising Sears and Kenmore together? The company increasingly saw its prices being undercut by discounters as customers insisted on shopping based on price instead of on brand loyalty. The only way Sears could maintain its sales against the competition was to offer a full range of choices.

> *Q: If you had a small appliance store offering exclusively Maytag appliances and saw places like Sears expanding to offer many different brands, what would you try to do to stay in business?*

14.17

Local television stations have been running many ads by Southwestern Bell, the regional local telephone company, for DSL lines. The reason for this deluge may be described by my household's behavior. We got rid of our second phone line, the one we had been using for a dial-up Internet connection, and had the TV cable company install a cable modem. DSL competes with cable modems, so Southwestern Bell lost business in its basic telephone line of operations when we made our decision. It also lost business in the growing market for fast Internet connections. The ads are its strategy to fight back in that market. Presumably it recognizes that the market for second telephone lines is not going to grow any more and realizes that it must expand its share of Internet connections.

> *Q: Currently, cable modems are much more widespread than DSL service. That being the case, what strategies beyond advertising would you recommend to Southwestern Bell to expand the DSL business?*

14.18

One of my students is active on eBay, where he sells autographed editions of CDs that he bought elsewhere. His current gimmick is a new CD recorded and autographed by Janet Jackson. Only fifty were sold initially nationwide, all at stores in New York City. My student is selling twelve on eBay, and his friend is selling nineteen. Together my student and his friend are almost **duopolists;** their problem is how to maintain collusion. The problem is enhanced by the fact that in a few days Janet Jackson will be signing 500 copies of this CD in stores. As that date approaches, and as potential customers discover that the supply of autographed CDs will be expanding greatly, the value of his twelve and his friend's nineteen will drop drastically. Each will have a tremendous incentive to cut prices in order to unload the inventory before its value plummets. It is difficult to reap **monopoly**—or even duopoly—profits, when customers realize that your monopoly or duopoly is about to end.

> *Q: The student only has five days left to unload the CDs. If you were in his position, how would you price them during this five-day period?*

14.19

The major fast-food chains seem to be unable to break the ninety-nine-cent barrier for burger prices. The standard burger price goes above $1 occasionally, and then one of the major companies begins selling "Value Meals" or the equivalent, and the others have to cut back prices to attract customers. This is classic "kinked demand curve" behavior: If you raise your price in an oligopoly and the others don't, you lose lots of sales. (If the market were competitive, you couldn't raise prices at all without losing all your sales.) Both Burger King and McDonald's are not making much profit from their most famous products, the Whopper and the Big Mac. Wendy's has followed a different strategy, going for the high end by marketing quality and charging more. This strategy has paid off: Wendy's profits have grown very sharply over the last five years. Why don't McDonald's and Burger King do the same thing? Perhaps because they have marketed at the middle or lower end for so long, their advertisements for high-quality, high-end products would not be credible.

> *Q: If McDonald's advertises a new "Superburger" costing the same as Wendy's products, would you believe an advertisement trumpeting its high quality? What could McDonald's do to get you to believe the ad?*

14.20

The federal government is seeking public comments on proposals that would allow airlines to impose surcharges on fares at peak business hours at the nation's busiest airports. Why don't the airlines just raise these fares themselves, since they are free to do so? The problem is that they often do try to raise fares, but without success. In the last two weeks, two airlines have successively tried to increase discount fares by $20 per ticket, only to back down when they found that the other **oligopolists** did not follow their price increases. If the oligopolists can get the government to state that raising fares is justified as a way of reducing congestion at busy times and places, it is more likely that airlines generally will go along with price increases. A government statement would provide the "cover" industry members need to justify raising their prices at the same time; it would prevent competition between them.

> *Q: Is the government serving consumers' interests if it makes this kind of statement? If not, why would the government do such a thing?*

14.21

Yale University is trying to get the federal government to allow it and other high-profile colleges and universities to collude to end their policy of early decision admissions. Under this policy, universities accept high school students in December of their senior year for entry the following September. This is a mechanism these elite schools use to compete for students. They don't like the outcome, and Yale and its colleagues are trying to end this policy. They argue that the universities admit early decision students who are not as well qualified as some students whom they might admit at the regular decision time in April. Why is this different from any other group of **oligopolists** seeking government protection to create a **monopoly** and protect the group against its members' inability to collude successfully? Yale claims that early decision hurts the student. Yet whenever a "firm" states that it wants to collude with other firms to help customers, observers wonder how unselfish its motives really are.

> *Q: If you were defending Yale University in an **antitrust** case arising out of its collusive behavior, how would you justify Yale's behavior as benefiting the public as a whole?*

14.22

All the big computer manufacturers—Dell, Gateway, Hewlett-Packard, IBM—have little "Intel Inside" logos (with their annoying five-note sound at the end) in their television advertisements. Intel subsidizes these advertisements if the companies include this logo. Other chip makers have urged **antitrust** agencies to restrict what they argue is simply a form of tied sale. **Tied sales**—a company's using its **monopoly** power in one market to enhance its position in another, competitive market—are generally illegal. Are Intel's **subsidies** a form of tying, or are they just rebates to the purchasers of chips? In both the United States and the European Union, these lawsuits have gone nowhere, with the antitrust agencies eventually dropping them. This rejection seems like a good policy decision: While Intel does have a huge share of the market for chips, there is no competitive market into which it is trying to spill over its monopoly power.

> *Q: Even though Intel may not be engaging in anticompetitive behavior by tying two products, can you argue that its behavior represents an anticompetitive practice in the chip market itself—an attempt to crowd out AMD, Cyrix, and the other small processor manufacturers? Or is it just a way of offering a volume discount to purchasers of the chips?*

14.23

Data for 2001 show that over 1 percent of medical doctors in Arizona were severely punished by the state licensing board for grave deficiencies in their practices. This is four times higher than the rate in neighboring California. Does this mean that Arizona contains an unusual number of bad doctors? If federal **antitrust** authorities prosecute more proposed corporate takeovers, does that mean that there is a trend toward monopolization? More generally, if a regulatory or government agency finds more malfeasance in an industry, what does it mean? The answer is: Nothing. The rate of malfeasance that is discovered depends on both the extent of underlying problems and the regulatory agency's persistence in finding and punishing people and firms. In considering differences in outcomes across states, where it is unlikely that underlying behavior differs very greatly, the role of government in searching for misbehavior is crucial. The same is true for variations over time in the extent of violations of federal regulations that are reported, because federal regulatory efforts vary greatly across presidential administrations.

Q: On your own campus, what would you conclude about a report that incidents of cheating are most common in, for example, engineering classes? Are engineering students more likely to cheat?

14.24

Tying-In the Dead. One of my sons tells me that his lawyer friend is suing a local Catholic church on behalf of a group of private stonemasons. The church owns cemeteries in his metropolitan area. Apparently, it will allow grave markers to be cut only by church-owned grave-marker companies. If you buy a plot in the Catholic cemetery, which is very attractive to religious Catholics, you must buy markers from specified outlets. This is a classic **tie-in sale:** The cemetery markets a monopolized product (the gravesites) and requires the purchaser to buy another product (the marker) in which it is one of many competitors. I would expect that this lawsuit will result in the church abandoning its tying policy, as courts generally rule they are illegal.

Q: If you were defending the church in this lawsuit, what eco-nomic arguments would you make in claiming that this practice should not be declared anticompetitive?

14.25

A colleague remarked that drugstores sell a product called Niagara that claims to have similar effects to the prescription drug Viagra. The product's name has now been changed to Nexcite. Numerous reasons led to the name change, but the main reason probably is that Niagara was sued or threatened with suit for trademark infringement by the manufacturer of the **monopolized** product Viagra. This is a pretty clear-cut case: The products are supposed to do the same thing, and a well-known trademark name is being appropriated to compete against its owner. But what if a new company in a totally different product market uses or refers to a trademark, in no way trying to compete in a legally monopolized market? One might argue that there's no problem, since there is no loss of sales by the company owning the trademark. The new company, though, is trying to make profits by using the older company's investment in its brand name. The owner doesn't lose anything in its original market, but the action is tantamount to stealing the fruits of someone else's investment.

Q: Johnny Carson, a popular television host in the 1970s and 1980s, was introduced every night by his sidekick yelling, "Here's Johnny!" During the 1980s, a portable toilet company used the phrase as the name for its product. Carson sued and succeeded in stopping the company from using this name. How is the Carson case different from the Niagara case? How is it the same?

14.26

The local newspaper reports that the U.S. Justice Department opposes allowing American Airlines and British Airways to ally in transatlantic travel, arguing that this will give them 51 percent of market share at London's Heathrow Airport. The airlines claim that the share would only be 37 percent and, more important, that the appropriate market is not just Heathrow, but all European hubs. They argue that those hubs, especially Paris and Frankfurt, are controlled by other U.S.–European airline alliances and that their own alliance will not give them a large share of the appropriately defined market: European hubs. This is a classic case of determining what the relevant market is in determining the potential effects of a merger.

Q: Give arguments to support the Justice Department's view that each local European hub constitutes a market. What evidence and data would you need to support that view?

Tips on Hunting for Economics Everywhere in Part 2

1. Look at how companies produce things—what techniques they use as they produce more—and how you and your friends choose to do different activities. When the cost of producing changes, look at how the method of production changes.
2. Consider whether fixed costs are ignored in deciding on a course of action for the present and the future. Is a company—or are you—behaving in a maximizing way?
3. Consider how the price of a good is determined by costs and by ease of entry into the market. Think about why the price of a competitively produced good might differ across geographical areas.
4. Look for shocks to markets. They are always occurring, both naturally and because of government actions. How do they affect price and quantity? How do changes in cost and technology affect price, quantity, and the size and number of suppliers?
5. Search for cases where people are dividing some fixed amount of anything. Can the group be made better off with a different division? If the amount changes, does the new distribution make everyone better off?
6. If there is only one supplier of a good or service, why? How is its monopoly protected? Does the monopolist take into account the impact of raising price on the quantity he or she sells?
7. Look for monopolists charging different prices for the same good or service. Why are they doing it—is it cost differences or differences in demand? How do they succeed in separating markets?
8. Look for suppliers colluding. Do they succeed? How do their strategies follow the ideas of game theory? Consider people's or companies' interactions in light of game theory.

PART 3

Input Markets,
the Public Sector,
and International Markets

CHAPTER 15

Discounting and Present Value

15.1

A young economist told me of her recent trip to Guanajuato, Mexico. Land is scarce there, so burial in the local cemetery need not be permanent. The heirs have a choice of paying for ten, thirty, sixty, or ninety years, or for permanent burial. Once the contract is paid, at the end of the specified time the deceased is dug up and cremated unless the lease is renewed. I wondered what the equilibrium price structure is. How much does the price rise as the length of time Grandpa is underground rises? The price should rise at a decreasing rate as the number of years rises, since *discounting* means that an extra year further in the future matters less, but one wonders whether people aren't willing to pay a big extra premium for knowing that Grandpa is buried safely for eternity. I would think that the price of keeping Grandpa underground for ninety years is less than three times as high as the thirty-year price, but that the "forever" price exceeds the ninety-year price by a lot.

> *Q: Does a simple **discount rate,** say, 3 percent per year, apply here? If people put a high weight on knowing that Grandpa is buried for good, how would you describe the rate at which they implicitly discount years far out in the future compared to years in the nearer term?*

15.2

A running race is really an economic problem, analogous to the problem a country faces with a fixed nonrenewable resource, such as coal, that it wants to mine at an optimal rate over time.

All runners have the problem of minimizing running time over the distance of a race. If they go out too fast, they poop out and wind up walking the last half of the race. If they conserve too much energy early in the race, they wind up with leftover strength near the end and are upset because they know they could have run the race faster. There is a correct rate at which to use one's physical reserves to get the best time, and it is related to the amount of resources, the depreciation rate, and the length of the **discounting period** (the race).

> *Q: Your rich uncle leaves you $10 million, and you know you can put it in the bank and get $500,000 in interest every year. Ask yourself: How much should I spend each year? (Remember, whatever you don't spend continues to get interest at 5 percent per year.)*

15.3

I have been running for exercise since 1967, in the early days averaging twenty-five miles a week, and these days twelve miles a week. Now my knees and hips hurt often. I always ran because I enjoyed it and thought it would be good for my long-term health. If I had known thirty-eight years ago how much my lower body would hurt (and how likely it is that someday I will need knee and/or hip replacements), would I have run so much? Is our *forward-looking maximizing behavior* the same as the behavior we would have undertaken if we knew the long-term consequences of our activities? Do we **discount** the future at too high a rate when we are young?

> *Q: How does this vignette apply to your behavior in timing your studying for economics over the semester? Give examples of cases in which your behavior implies that you discount the future at a very high rate.*

15.4

California is considering banning teenagers from using tanning salons. The argument is that their using the salons will increase the incidence of skin cancer, especially its deadly form, melanomas, many years in the future when the teens are in late middle age. For economists, the question is whether the teens have a sufficiently low **discount rate** that they will properly account for their future risk of getting skin cancer when they decide whether to go tanning now. If they do, then they will make a correct choice in comparing today's pleasures from being tan to the future risk of skin cancer and its costs. If not, and if the government is better at accounting for these future risks, banning teens from tanning salons makes economic sense. Judging by the teens whose behavior I have observed closely (my sons), I doubt that teenagers' discount rates are low enough to account for these future risks. So banning tanning by teens seems like a good idea.

Q: Short of banning tanning, what could you do so that teens account more fully for the future risks that their current actions will cause?

15.5

A (pretty bad) joke on the "Economist Joke" Web site (www.etla.fi/pkm/JokEc.html) goes, "I knew that economics was ruling my life when I tried to calculate my three-year-old son's **discount rate** by seeing how many sweets he would require to be promised to him after dinner to be equivalent to one sweet before dinner." Little kids discount the future at a very high rate. Let's say that the three-year-old is willing to give up one sweet before dinner in exchange for two sweets after dinner two hours later. That **trade-off** postpones gratification for one-twelfth of a day, or 1/4,380 of a year. The kid is insisting that his interest rate—the rate at which he discounts the future—is huge, far more than a trillion trillion percent per year. Kids are very impatient.

Q: Would the kid's implied interest rate be the same if the choice was $1 now or some amount of money after dinner? That is, would he insist on $2 after dinner, or might he settle for less after dinner?

15.6

Last night I went out to dinner at an excellent Mexican restaurant. I couldn't resist the frozen margarita, the enchiladas in mole sauce, and the *crepas de cajeta*, crepes in a caramel type of sauce. They taste so good, but I knew that I would not feel so great in the morning. Sure enough, I was awake at 4:30 AM with an upset stomach. As happens all too often, even though I know the consequences, when making the decision to eat I discounted those future consequences so heavily that the current enjoyment more than justified eating the good food. Regrettably, at 4:30 AM the enjoyment had worn off, and I was bemoaning my high **discount rate.**

Q: A similar example is a hangover, which should be fully expected if you drink too much. You know you'll get a hangover, and you keep drinking. What does that behavior, and the behavior in this vignette, tell you about your discount rate for the near future (the pleasure of tonight's drinking) versus the pain of tomorrow's hangover?

15.7

Yesterday's local paper gave some remarkably bad advice about lottery winnings. The columnist was asked about Lotto winnings when one chooses the cash option (all the money at once) or the twenty-five equal annual payments option. She responded, "If you selected the cash option for a $100 million jackpot, you would receive about one half the money . . . Then 25 percent for taxes is taken out. Your check would be $37.5 million. If you selected the annual payment option, you would receive considerably more— 25 annual payments, less the 25 percent income tax. Each payment would be about $3 million [totaling about $75 million]." Now each sentence here is correct. But the columnist makes it sound like the annual payment option gives you much more. It gives you more dollars, but it gives you dollars in the future, up through twenty-five years from now. When you take the **present discounted value** of those dollars, you find that the annual payment option yields a present value exactly equal to the cash option. So which one should you take? That depends on how badly you want the dollars now. If you are impatient—if $.95 today is worth more to you than $1 next year—you should take the cash option; if not, go for the annual payment option. Most lottery winners take the cash now—they are pretty impatient.

Q: How should your choice between the two options be affected if the Lotto suddenly figures the interest rate is 20 percent per year and discounts the cash value amount accordingly?

15.8

My daughter-in-law scheduled arthroscopic surgery on her knee. Surgery is an investment for her and in many other cases: There is no doubt that you are more debilitated after the surgery than you were before. Presumably, you do it because eventually you'll be in better shape than you were before; thus, the **present discounted value** of the improvements exceeds the current cost. If you are quite old, the ailment is not too serious or restrictive, or the surgery is very invasive, it doesn't make sense to have it done. Even if the ailment isn't too serious and the surgery is very difficult, it could well make sense to do it if you are young and can envision many years of perfect health after the recovery period.

> *Q: What if the issue is not surgery, but instead six months of very painful treatment for a cancer that currently is causing you no physical problems but that is potentially fatal (even though the chance of it being fatal is only 3 percent)? Would you take the treatment?*

15.9

February 8, 2002—I don't want to kick people when they are down, nor do I want to be nasty, but did the Enron employees who claim to have lost millions in retirement funds really lose that much? The appropriate way to think about their loss is not to compare the value of their Enron stock today (nearly zero) with what it was near its peak in January 2001 ($83 per share). Why should we feel sorry for them to the tune of what they would have had at the artificially inflated value of the stock at its peak? The appropriate measure of their loss is what the investment in their pensions (along with whatever Enron paid in for them) would have been worth if they had been receiving a normal rate of return from the time the money was invested. If, for example, someone put in $10,000 at the start of 1997, it would have risen to $43,000 by the end of 2000, but the loss is *not* $43,000. Instead, a reasonable measure of the loss, assuming a 10 percent rate of return over the four-year period, is $10,000*[1.1]^4 = $14,641, far smaller than the amount the Enron employees claim.

> *Q: The Enron employees might well argue, "But we had the $43,000, we had planned on having it for retirement, and now you're only giving us $14,641. We have lost." How would you respond to that argument?*

15.10

My mother-in-law undertook the trauma of moving from Boston to Austin at age 86. She died exactly six months after she moved. The move took a lot of my mother-in-law's time and my wife's time, and it cost some money. Even though the **discounting period** (the time she spent in Austin) was sadly very short, in retrospect these costs were more than offset by the benefits of her being in Texas. She liked Austin a lot, seemed much happier with her environment; and we enjoyed having her here, seeing a lot more of her than we otherwise would have. If the per-period benefit of an investment is large enough, that investment will pay off even with a very short discounting period.

Q: How would we have felt about the move if she had died the day after she moved? How about if she had lived ten more years?

15.11

Fixing Fluffy and Fido. The city of Houston gives a $15 discount on your pet license if the pet has been neutered. Ignoring whether you enjoy a neutered pet more or less than a natural one, is neutering a good investment? Say it costs $100 to have Fido neutered. This will yield a stream of savings of $15 per year as long as Fido lives. But the returns are in the future, and Fido isn't going to live forever. Even with a zero percent interest rate, he has to live six and two-thirds years to make the investment worthwhile. If the interest rate is 5 percent, he has to live over eight years; if it's 10 percent, he has to live eleven years. The city is offering an economic incentive, but it doesn't seem to be a very large one given the length of the **discounting period.**

Q: Using each of these interest rates, calculate how long the dog or cat has to live if the discount on the pet license is increased to $20 and the cost of neutering is $100.

CHAPTER 16

*L*abor Markets

Labor Demand and Supply

16.1

A story in a Washington newspaper reports on a lawsuit brought by violinists in the Beethoven Orchestra in Bonn, Germany. The violinists are arguing that they should be paid more than other orchestra members, since they play more notes per concert than other musicians. Since they work more than their wind-instrument colleagues, they believe that they deserve higher pay. I would be surprised if they succeed—nor should they. The relevant measure of their output is their **marginal revenue product,** the amount that their playing adds to revenue. Moreover, if violinists are plentiful and, for example, flautists are scarce, no orchestra will be spending its budget wisely if it pays more to violinists than to flautists (although it would have an incentive to put additional string symphonies into its concert programs). The violinists in Bonn do not seem to understand how labor markets work.

> *Q: The violinists are using what economists call the **"labor theory of value."** How would you apply this same idea to arguing for a higher grade in your economics class?*

16.2

Life is getting tougher for European soccer heroes. In the mid-1990s, a boom began in transfers of players among teams, which had previously been very difficult. The easing of transfers resulted in bidding wars for the biggest stars, and European soccer players' salaries skyrocketed. By 2003, however, the bidding war had slowed down, mainly because audiences were no long as interested in watching soccer on television as they had been earlier.

Television revenues increase the **marginal revenue product of labor,** enhancing the players' value and, in a competitive labor market, enabling players to command higher salaries. With the slowdown in revenue growth, the marginal revenue product is no longer growing and may be declining. Players who had hoped to command increasingly large salaries for their skills are disappointed with what they receive. Of course, the players are still earning much, much more than they would have earned before restrictions on transfers among teams were eased—and even more than their **opportunity cost** outside of soccer-playing.

Q: Compare this description to what happened in major league baseball beginning in the late 1970s, and examine what has happened to baseball salaries over the past 10 years.

16.3

Is it better to hire someone who will do barely enough with certainty or someone who might be great or might be a disaster? Do we really choose to hire those potential employees whose expected **marginal revenue product** is above their wage rate? If we can hire as many workers as we want, that textbook approach is correct. But what if you are limited in the number you can hire? And what if you can fire the workers who turn out to be duds, which is true in most nonunion workplaces in the United States? In that case, it pays to look not only at the amount that you expect the worker to produce, but also at the maximum that she or he might generate for the company. This is evident in hiring new faculty members. We can always deny lifetime tenure to those who turn out to be mediocre; we can fire them after a probationary period of six years. And we gain prestige from those who end up doing really important research. With that reward structure in universities, it pays to choose a riskier faculty member—one who might bomb or who might produce Nobel Prize–winning research—over a competent plodder who offers no risks. The same considerations apply in any business where individual productivity matters a lot and where the company chooses between two workers it expects to be equally productive on average.

Q: What would happen in this situation if the government passed a law requiring universities to grant tenure or fire the faculty after a shorter probationary period, say, only three years? How should our decision change?

16.4

Very few industrialized labor markets today are characterized by **monopsony:** It's easy for an exploited worker in a metropolitan area to get a job elsewhere. This wasn't always the case, though. Saul David, in *The Indian Mutiny: 1857* (New York: Viking, 2002) discusses the so-called Sepoy Rebellion, in which soldiers employed by the East India Company, which controlled India for the British Empire, staged a very bloody revolt. Historians have viewed the revolt as being over religious issues or as an early nationalist uprising. David takes the novel view that the Sepoys wanted to encourage independence by local maharajahs as a way of guaranteeing job advancement and generating competition for their service—and, thus, higher pay. By breaking the power of the monopsonistic East India Company, they would be able to encourage the independent maharajahs to compete among themselves and bid up the price of the hired soldiers.

Q: How is the Sepoys' behavior like that of the European soccer players discussed in Vignette 16.2?

16.5

Newsweek quoted Keith Richards, explaining why tickets to shows on the "final" Rolling Stones world tour cost much more than tickets to see Sir Paul McCartney: "There's more of us." Richards implicitly believes in the Marxian **"labor theory of value"**—that the price of a product is determined by the amount of the labor input in production. Labor costs matter, but they aren't the only thing that matters. Indeed, in this case the tickets probably cost more simply because there is more demand to see the entire Rolling Stones group than to see a single Beatle. It's the greater demand that allows the Stones to charge a higher price than Sir Paul—and that makes their current ticket prices exceed his.

Q: A ticket to see Simon and Garfunkel recently cost only half of my ticket to see the Stones. Is this because the Stones consist of four main players, while S & G are only two people?

16.6

The Nakednews Channel, a Web-based service, presents news broadcasts, including foreign events, domestic events, business news, sports, and weather, by newscasters who are entirely naked. One wonders if the high pay of anchorpersons on the regular news channels isn't more for their looks than for their journalistic acumen. Nakednews takes this phenomenon one step further. What will happen to news anchors' pay if the naked phenomenon takes over television journalism entirely? Instead of merely having an ability to read the news well and look halfway decent from the shoulders up, news anchors also will need to look good fully unclothed. (This may present problems for Jennings and Williams.) Fewer people will qualify to be network news anchors, and the **superstars** among tomorrow's naked anchors will receive even higher pay than is received by today's clothed news anchors.

Q: What would the widespread acceptance of Nakednews do to the relationship between wages and age in the television business?

16.7

An economist has tabulated **revenue** from ticket sales at rock concerts in each of the last twenty years. Total ticket revenue has grown rapidly. The top 1 percent and top 5 percent of bands have received increasing shares of total revenue: There has been increasing inequality in band revenue. This has paralleled the growth in income inequality over this period. It may be due to the phenomenon of **superstars.** As concert venues get larger and more fans become familiar with the top groups through MTV and other sources that allow the biggest names to expand their markets, the top groups can reap sharply increased revenue. The lesser groups still have fans and do OK, explaining why total revenue in the industry has risen.

Q: What do you think will happen to inequality of rock bands' ticket sales if downloading music from the Internet becomes easier?

16.8

A graduating senior comes to talk about the course and about what he's going to do after graduation. He's thinking of getting an M.A. degree next year. He reasons that the job market is currently very tight, so that the **opportunity cost** of being in grad school will be low, because it would be hard for him to find a job. He figures that in a year the job market will be better, and he will be well positioned to get a good job with his new advanced degree. Maybe he's right. But a lot of studies suggest that if everybody thinks this way, the market becomes glutted with newly degreed people. They all entered grad school thinking they would earn a lot on graduation. When they come out on the job market, the large supply of new graduates drives down their earnings. My student may be in for a rude surprise.

Q: So how should you time grad school? If you go during good times, you give up job opportunities now, but you have fewer competing graduates when you finish your program. Is that a better or a worse choice for you than the choice outlined in the vignette?

16.9

We had two choices for an assisted-living facility (all meals provided along with some personal services) for my mother-in-law. The less expensive one has bigger apartments, is three years newer, and has a better location than the more expensive one. We chose the more expensive one. The reason is that the marketing person at the physically nicer one admitted that they regularly lose employees to the one we chose. We've also heard from friends that the staff at the place we chose is extremely gentle and caring toward the residents. The reason it is more expensive is that it pays its workers more. The higher wages attract a higher-quality staff, but the costs have to be passed on to the consumer in this competitive market.

Q: Look at the part-time jobs your fellow students have. Is there a relationship between how much they earn and your perception of their potential quality as employees?

16.10

February 13, 2002—Derek Parra, the American ice skater who won an Olympic silver medal this week, grew up in southern California, not the usual locale for ice-skating champions. Parra was a champion in-line skater who wanted to go to the Olympics but couldn't, because in-line skating is not an Olympic event. He was persuaded to try ice skating, and his skills were readily transferable to this more established sport. If in-line skating did not exist, Parra would not be an Olympic ice skater. This is a case in which technological change (the development of in-line skating, which did not occur until the 1980s) enabled a wide range of people to develop skills that are easily transferred to a different activity (ice skating). How many other new technologies (perhaps video games) have enabled people to develop skills that enhance their productivity in older, more established activities?

> *Q: Give other examples of these kinds of complementary skills. For example, how might skills honed playing pool be transferable to one's activity as a batter in baseball?*

Equilibrium in the Labor Market

16.11

We're taking four grandchildren to Storybook Land, an ancient amusement park in central New Jersey. It is open all week in summers and on weekends during the rest of the year. I notice that all the workers in the park seem to be under age twenty or over age sixty. Why? With a market catering to young schoolchildren, the park would not be profitable on weekdays except in the summer—demand would be insufficient to cover the **variable cost** of keeping the park open. The park couldn't offer full-year full-time jobs, so that most prime-age adult workers, who seek full-time jobs, would find other employment more attractive. But the schedule is ideal for retirees and for high school or college students. The park attracts workers in these age brackets because it **matches** the schedule on which the park can stay open and make a profit with the preferences of this particular group of workers.

> *Q: My high-school English teacher was also the door-to-door milk deliveryman in summers. Was his doing this consistent with the idea expressed in this vignette? In what other occupations would you expect to observe adult workers taking this kind of job?*

16.12

Because my undergraduate econometrics class has sixty students, I do not have the time to deal with each student in developing the short term paper that I require. Instead, I am asking students to work in pairs. The **matching** of students to form these pairs is an interesting example of two-sided matching, something that economists have studied in a variety of entry-level job markets. If all that matters is getting the best grade on the term paper with the minimum of effort, each student will want to match with the best student (in terms of both ability and willingness to work) in the class. If the best student is already matched, the remaining students presumably will want to match with the next-best student, and so on. If there is perfect information about each student's ability, the equilibrium will be the optimal one for eliciting performance: The top student will match with the next-best, students 3 and 4 will match, and so on. Unfortunately, information is far from perfect, and factors other than expected performance may enter into matching decisions. Regrettably, I expect to have a number of pairs where one student winds up doing almost all the work.

> *Q: How is the matching process described here affected if I allow some students to write a paper alone (without any co-worker)? Now consider matching in the market for spouses. How does the two-sided matching in that market resemble that in the "market" for paper coauthors? What is the equivalent in the marriage market of a student writing a paper alone? How does it affect the equilibrium matching in that market?*

16.13

People engage in job searches; they also search for spouses through dating and other activities. They will search more if the dispersion of the outcomes they might obtain (the quality of the jobs or the quality of the marriage partners) is greater. In the last three decades, a tremendous decline has taken place in marriage rates in the United States. Over this time period, inequality of earnings among men has risen sharply. It pays a woman who is searching in the marriage market to postpone marriage when inequality among men is greater, because the benefits from waiting longer to find "Mr. Right" are greater when he differs more from the average guy the woman might find. Two economists have shown that the age at which women marry has risen most rapidly in cities where inequality among men's earnings has risen the most. Rational search described changes in American women's marriage patterns in the late twentieth century, and it probably still does. This isn't the only cause of later marriages: Better job opportunities for women matter a lot, but changing incentives to search in the marriage market have led women to postpone marriage.

> *Q: African-American men's earnings inequality has risen more than that of whites. What do you think has happened to the marriage rate among African-American women?*

16.14

A professor of French literature was complaining about the high salaries paid to economics professors at this university and other universities. He is a competent researcher and teacher, has a Ph.D., and has twenty years of experience, yet he makes less than the new Ph.D. graduates we are hiring to start their teaching and research careers. He viewed this difference as absurd. Why should he with his skills be paid less? His job is no more fun than mine; he's not giving up any pay because he enjoys his work much more than economics professors enjoy theirs. He's paid less because of supply and demand in a competitive labor market. A lot of people want to be French professors relative to universities' demand for them, and relatively few want to be economics professors compared to the demand for them. The difference arises because there are many jobs outside college teaching for economists and people who might become economists. To maintain an economics faculty, universities have to compete for talent. Alternative employment opportunities for would-be French professors are few. This is sad because we're really doing the same job. But if a university went ahead and paid equally, lowering economists' pay and raising French professors' pay, it would have a great French faculty and a dreadful bunch of economists. No competent economist would want to come to such a university, and the ones already there would soon leave for greener pastures.

> *Q: If you were a university president and wanted to maintain the quality of the faculty in all your fields without having a large budget, what, if anything, could you do to satisfy the French professor in this example?*

16.15

Government statistics show that in Texas beauticians earn $12.42 per hour while barbers earn only $9.58, a ratio of 1.30. But in California, beauticians earn $9.96 per hour and barbers earn $8.74, a ratio of 1.14. Why is the relative wage of beauticians so much higher in Texas? Are the wage differentials caused by demand or supply forces? A sensible supply-side explanation is that being a beautician in Texas is harder work than being a beautician in California. Texas women are famous for "big hair," and generating big hair requires more effort and skill, and more time, than does giving an ordinary haircut of the kind that may be more common in California. Also, Texas men are more likely to have "buzz cuts" than are California surfer dudes. Since it's less difficult to give a buzz cut, the skills required of Texas barbers may be less than those required of California barbers. It's hard to think of a demand-side explanation that works this well. Even if demand for beauticians doing the same work that is done elsewhere were much higher in Texas, in the long run more workers in Texas would become beauticians than elsewhere. That would drive beauticians' wages back to the national equilibrium.

Q: *If the wage of beauticians is so much higher in Texas, why don't California beauticians migrate to Texas and increase their wages by 25 percent?*

16.16

A nightclub pianist views his most dangerous job hazards as "Piano Man," "My Brown-Eyed Girl," and "American Pie." He hates playing them because he is asked to play them so often. He notes, however, that if a customer pays him $20, he'll play anything the customer wants, even these songs. **Compensating wage differentials** arise in employment but also in jobs that rely on tips. At some extra wage people will do a lot of things on the job that they would otherwise (for no or very little extra pay) find repugnant and refuse to do.

Q: *If you work or have ever worked for pay, which things on your job do you find to be the most repugnant? How much pay per hour would you be willing to give up if you didn't have to do them?*

16.17

You Think You've Got a Bad Job! A report on BBC World discussed the problems of gatherers of wild honey in the mangrove forests of Bangladesh. This is an extremely risky job—not because of problems with the bees that produce the honey—they're pretty harmless. The problem is with tigers that live in the swamps and that like to eat the honey (and also unfortunately the honey-gatherers whom they confront). Indeed, in the past summer alone tigers ate two of the roughly 400 honey-gatherers. Why would anyone take this kind of risk, a 0.5 percent chance each year of being killed on the job? The reason is that a honey gatherer can earn in three months what an agricultural laborer earns in a year. This 400 percent wage premium (a monthly wage four times that in agriculture) is a sufficient **compensating wage differential** to induce workers to face an annual risk of on-the-job death of 0.5 percent, far higher than the risk in any occupation in the United States.

> *Q: Look up in official government statistics which kinds of jobs in the United States have the highest risk of death on the job. What do you expect to observe about wages paid for such work?*

16.18

The life of a clergyperson—minister, rabbi, or whatever—seems very difficult. It's not the sermonizing or leading religious services, but rather the need to minister to families at times of grave personal stress: divorce, serious illness, or death. You would think that it would take a high wage—a large **compensating wage differential**—to draw people into the profession. In fact, if you adjust for everything that you might think affects earnings—education, age, location, race, sex, ethnicity, hours of work, and so on—male clergy in the United States earn less than 60 percent of what otherwise identical workers earn. Why? It has to be that there are enough people who enjoy helping other people at difficult times and are willing to work in a very low-paid occupation. Without that kind of willingness for self-sacrifice—without people who have a "calling" to the ministry—we would quickly be unable to attract enough people into this occupation to fill all the pulpits in a religious country like the United States.

> *Q: What would happen to the wage of clergy, compared to other college graduates, if the government launched an advertising campaign to get more people to become ministers, rabbis, and priests?*

16.19

The federal government regulates how American companies pay health and pension benefits to their employees. It imposes large penalties on a company that offers bigger benefits to highly paid employees than it offers to its lower-paid workers. A recent study shows how companies respond. In companies whose employees are more heterogeneous and, thus, where the federal regulation has a bigger effect on the benefits offered, wages are more dispersed. The federal penalty creates an incentive for employers to avoid offering extra benefits to unusually highly skilled workers. To offset the lower benefits compared to what other companies might offer, the companies instead offer them a **compensating wage differential** that helps attract and retain them. Those companies also respond by placing more of their low-skilled workers on part-time status—a smart move, since part-time workers' benefits are not regulated under this federal mandate. As in most cases, prices (in this case, wages) and quantities partly adjust to a government-imposed regulation.

> *Q: Another federal regulation in the labor market is that overtime (hours after forty hours per week) must be paid at time-and-a-half. How does this regulation change hourly wage rates in companies that offer a lot of overtime compared to companies that never offer overtime work?*

16.20

The song "Proud Mary" by Creedence Clearwater Revival begins, "Left a good job in the city, workin' for the Man every night and day." This is a really silly sentence. If the person was working "every night and day," it couldn't have been "a good job." That implies many hours of work each week. In the United States, only a small fraction of workers put in more than fifty hours per week, many of them self-employed professionals and highly paid managers, not the kind of person who might be singing this song. Also, if the person worked at night, it is unlikely that the job was good: Nighttime work is most common among workers with few skills and low wages. It is also more prevalent among workers in minority groups that are discriminated against. Night work pays better than comparable day work—there is a **compensating wage differential** for night work—but not much better. Work at night is typically undesirable work.

> *Q: Find a want ad for a nighttime job. Look at the wage being offered and compare it to a want ad for a similar job with a daytime schedule.*

16.21

The big story on campus is the appearance of several University of Texas students in *Playboy*'s feature "Girls of the Big 12." One of the students who is featured was quoted in the local newspaper later as noting that some of the women in the article kept their clothes on: "That's so not fair. I hope they didn't get paid for wearing those skirts." In fact, *Playboy* paid the unclothed women $500, but paid less to those who were seminude, and paid even less for fully clothed pictures. In the market for supplying such pictures, the offer price rises as the amount revealed increases (since revealing more requires a **compensating wage differential**). Five hundred dollars seems like a pretty low price, but it reflects sorting: Most women would not do this at $500, but enough are willing that the market demand can be satisfied with *Playboy* offering a price of only $500.

> *Q: What would happen to the price that* Playboy *would be willing to offer if the fraction of homosexuals among the male population increased?*

Economic Rent

16.22

Listening to Mick Jagger sing "Satisfaction" today reminded me of my favorite example of **economic rent**: two guys, each sixty-one years old, each having majored in economics in college, each running long-distance for exercise, and each having a child who graduated from Yale. The two guys are Mick Jagger and me. We probably have the same **opportunity cost**: For both of us, the alternative uses of our time aren't great. Both of us earn more than our opportunity cost, but Mick earns much more than I do, so he is receiving much more economic rent than I am. The British or American government could tax Mick's music earnings a lot, and he would still be willing to continue singing. If they imposed a huge tax on my earnings from economics, they'd be taxing away more than my economic rent, and I'd quit teaching economics.

> *Q: Let's say I earn $100,000 as an economist, and my next-best alternative is as a singer earning $20,000. How much could the government tax away without me leaving economics to become a singer?*

16.23

Until 1975, the federal National Institutes of Health (NIH) identified young scientists and offered them career-long financial support (salary only) to do research at their own university laboratories. Only ten such grants were in force at any time. The NIH discovered that about half the scientists continued to do good research over most of their lifetimes, while the other half soon stopped doing serious research and happily enjoyed their sinecures. To someone who thinks economic considerations dominate everything, the surprising fact is that half the scientists continued to work productively. Financial incentives do matter, and no doubt that is why the NIH abolished the program and replaced it with five-year renewable grants. But nonfinancial incentives—the desire to excel, the desire to avoid embarrassment, and the love of one's work—provide an important spur, too. For people who are motivated by these incentives, the financial rewards are at least partly **economic rent** to an activity they would pursue even at lower pay.

> *Q: Michael Jordan made $40 million per year playing basketball and endorsing products. If the government taxed away $35 million, would Michael still have played basketball and done product endorsements? How much of his $40 million earnings is economic rent?*

16.24

This winter, American Airlines is offering extra mileage on frequent-flyer accounts if you buy round-trip tickets to Europe. For the first round-trip this winter, you get 5,000 miles of credit; you get 15,000 miles for two trips, and 30,000 miles for three trips. The purpose presumably is to induce people to buy tickets during a period when demand is low. But I had booked three flights to Europe even before this offer came out, so the incentive had no effect on my decisions to travel. For me, the 30,000 extra frequent-flyer miles (enough to get one free domestic ticket) are **economic rent**—they could be withdrawn with no effect on my choices about whether or not to fly.

> *Q: Among the jobs you have held, which one has given you the greatest amount of economic rent?*

CHAPTER 17

*H*uman Capital, Discrimination, and Labor-Market Policy

Education and Training

17.1

At the urging of many citizens and members of the legislature, my university is considering abandoning or minimizing its use of SAT scores in admissions. The University of California has already greatly reduced its use of test scores. Is this a good idea? At my university, a study of a large random sample of graduates shows that within the same major and separately by gender, and adjusting for how well students performed in high school, those with higher SAT scores when they applied had higher GPAs at graduation from the university. Each extra 100 SAT points adds 0.12 extra GPA points. For example, going from 1,100 to 1,200 raises GPA from 3.00 to 3.12. SAT shouldn't be the sole criterion for admission, but the fact that it offers independent evidence on how well a student will perform in college means that the information it provides should not be entirely ignored, since it indicates how productive investments in **human capital** might be.

> *Q: If, instead of abandoning SAT scores in admission, the university decides to stop using high school rank, would the kinds of students—race, sex, and so on—admitted to the university be any different? If you must abandon SAT or high school rank, which one should be dropped?*

17.2

A report on CNN states, "Ten years ago only 16 percent of the highest-income families borrowed for college. By 2000 that had grown to 45 percent." This should not be surprising, and it doesn't indicate that today's higher-income families are poverty-stricken. It's a rational response to changing costs and benefits. The costs of borrowing to finance a college education are fairly low today because interest rates are far below what they were in the 1980s. The returns of going to college—the return on the investment in **human capital** that is represented by time in college and a college degree—far exceed the costs of borrowing. It makes sense to borrow when the returns exceed the costs, and that's just what students are doing. Students are doing exactly the right thing given the incentives the market is providing.

> *Q: If you did not take out student loans, why not? If you did, could you have borrowed more? If yes, why didn't you borrow more?*

17.3

One of the students offered a particularly clear example of **investment in human capital,** in the form of on-the-job training. Pilots are willing to fly for very low wages in small regional carriers or other low-paying aircraft operators. Indeed, the student claims that her flight instructor believes that some pilots are willing to fly for nothing, although in fact the employer does pay them at least the minimum wage. The inexperienced pilots are willing to do this as a way of accumulating the skills that will enable them to qualify for high-paying pilot jobs at larger airlines. They give up some earning power initially. They do this because they hope eventually to obtain the returns of much higher earnings at the better jobs for which the training will qualify them.

> *Q: Some new law school graduates take one-year jobs as clerks for federal judges, earning perhaps $40,000 per year at the same time that their classmates take jobs in large law firms earning over $100,000 per year. Why do these people take such relatively low-paid positions?*

17.4

We were talking about the news that Iran may be paying $25,000 to the families of suicide bombers. A colleague remarked that this is probably the entire present value of their lifetime earnings: the value of their **human capital.** This is reminiscent of a calculation an economist did in the early 1960s. After the Bay of Pigs debacle—the failed attempt to take over Cuba in 1961, shortly after Fidel Castro had assumed power—the prisoners Castro had captured were exchanged for tractors and medicine. The economist showed that the market price of this material, $53 million, was very close to the value of the 1,113 prisoners' human capital—the discounted value of their lifetime earnings. Castro, by now one of the last communist leaders, had a good intuitive grasp of market economics early in his career.

> *Q: What would happen to the amount Castro was paid if the prisoners were all men age sixty?*

17.5

State legislators in a number of states are proposing that college athletes be paid several hundred dollars a month by their universities. Major football programs can certainly afford this small payment, but should payments be made? A college athlete may be spending his or her time just for the enjoyment of the sport, but many are making an investment in developing their **human capital** in the form of athletic skills. This is a very risky investment. Most athletes won't recoup anything—they'll never make the pro leagues—but a very few will strike it phenomenally rich. Since nobody forces college athletes to go to college, or to engage in athletics, one must assume that the college athletes make the choice freely. The only argument in favor of paying them might be that they don't understand how few athletes find that the investment pays off—how risky the investment is. If that's true—if the market is noncompetitive because information about the risks is lacking—the prescription should be better information, not a required payment for the athletes.

> *Q: You are asked to develop information for college athletes on the risks of spending much of their college life engaged in sports training. What specific information would you list to illustrate the risks, and benefits, of a college sporting career?*

17.6

The newly unionized union of lecturers (temporary faculty) at the University of Michigan is threatening a strike if their wage and other demands are not met. One of their demands is a minimum salary of $40,000 for nine months of teaching by an inexperienced lecturer, with the minimum to rise by 5 percent per year of experience. That would mean that a lecturer who is kept on for twenty years would receive $80,000, more than most full professors at the two outlying University of Michigan campuses (Flint and Dearborn). Is 5 percent higher wages per year of experience unusual? Absolutely; while workers may average increases this big, they are partly due to inflation, partly due to economic growth economywide. If we examine how wages vary with workers' experience at a point in time, we see that they are about 3 percent higher with the first year of experience, and the extra earnings that you get with each additional year of experience drops as you accumulate more experience. The reason is that the increases result from investment in **human capital** in the form of **on-the-job training,** investments that diminish as workers gain experience. The annual increase in your skills slows down as you have accumulated more skills. The lecturers union is asking for something that just doesn't exist in the real world.

    Q: Is there ever a point where lower wages to the most senior workers compared to somewhat younger workers might be justified? What would be the justification?

17.7

When our younger son was fifteen, my wife finished law school and began practicing as an attorney. I had already been working as a professor for eighteen years. I told my son that I was tired of arguing with him about increasing his allowance and that, henceforth, we would index it—it would increase each year by the same percentage amount as my pay would rise. He immediately said, "Dad, I want my allowance indexed to Mom's wage increases." I thought about this and realized that this fifteen-year-old understood **human capital** theory and the nature of investment in **on-the-job training.** He knew that, early in their careers, people's wages increase rapidly, because they are learning a lot in their job, but that people who have been working in the same job for a long time do not see such rapid increases. Unfortunately for him, I understood the theory, too, and told him, "Sorry, Buster—your allowance will be indexed to increases in my salary, not Mom's!"

Q: Given this indexing rule, how did my son feel about how I should spend my work time?

17.8

Mary Chapin Carpenter's song "He Thinks He'll Keep Her" tells of a woman who has three children in quick succession, stays home to take care of them, and then gets divorced at age thirty-six. Thereafter, "For fifteen years she had a job and not one raise in pay, now she's in the typing pool at **minimum wage**." If she was working in the labor market, I doubt that she had no raise in pay for fifteen years. But that she didn't earn very much is not surprising. During the time of life when most people are investing in **human capital** in the form of **on-the-job training,** she stayed home. Her marketable skills didn't grow, and whatever skills she had before she got married depreciated. Wage growth represents a return to investment in human capital, and the skills learned on the job represent a large part of every worker's human capital.

Q: If you don't plan to start working until age thirty-five, what kinds of occupations should you train for? What college majors would be appealing?

Discrimination

17.9

Leviticus 27 begins with a set of valuations of the productivity of people of different ages and sexes. It contains the famous valuation of women ages twenty through sixty as being worth 30 shekels, and men ages twenty through sixty being worth 50 shekels. Boys ages five through twenty are worth 20 shekels, girls five through twenty worth 10 shekels. Old men (sixty+) are worth 15 shekels, old women worth 10 shekels. These valuations look amazingly like wage differences today. The highest wage is for prime-age men; the growth in valuations and wages between young men and prime-age men is steepest; and the decline in valuations between prime-age and old men is the sharpest. The growth and decline are less sharp for women, so that gender differences in wage levels are largest among people ages twenty through sixty.

Q: Go on the Web and try to find out what the average wage is for men and women nationwide. Then get information on this wage difference for college-age youths, for people in their thirties and forties, and for those in their sixties.

17.10

If you ever attend a play or concert, you notice that the lines for women's restrooms are almost always longer than those for men's restrooms. This is no doubt a result of basic biological and cultural differences that guarantee that with the same number of usable toilets, women's waits will be longer. The question is whether this is fair: Are facilities discriminating when they contain restrooms that guarantee that women will have to wait longer? A number of states have responded by enacting "toilet **equity**" laws, requiring in some cases that the average waiting times be equal (which requires more women's than men's toilets). Whether these laws make sense depends on whether you believe that no **discrimination** means equality of access or equality of outcomes. The issue thus mirrors the general question of discrimination in education, labor markets, and other areas. Is it opportunity or outcomes that should concern us? In this case, do we mean access in terms of number or access in terms of time spent?

Q: How do you respond to the argument that it makes sense for women to wait in bathroom lines longer, since the average women's time is less valuable than the average man's if we measure the value of time by market wages?

17.11

A woman weighing 240 pounds conducts an aerobics class in San Francisco. The woman had been denied a job by a for-profit fitness center. She sued under San Francisco law, which prohibits **discrimination** based on appearance, arguing that she had been leading aerobics classes for fifteen years. Was she being discriminated against because of her weight? In other words, was this pure discrimination? Or was she not hired because her potential employer felt that her weight would ensure that few or no clients would take her classes? Was this a sound commercial decision based on her likely productivity? It is impossible to decide between these two possibilities, and this is true generally in cases where the source of potential bias is consumer preferences. The same arguments can be made about discrimination against minorities or women: Businesspeople could always rationalize a refusal to hire on grounds that hiring would be bad for business. If determining the underlying cause is so difficult, in the end we have to decide which groups to protect on political, not economic, grounds.

> *Q: Give arguments in favor of protecting the overweight against discrimination of this kind. Then give arguments against protecting them.*

17.12

Economists in the United States and elsewhere have studied the wages of gay and lesbian workers in comparison to those of other workers. One study deals with the Netherlands. The research shows that after adjusting for things such as age, education, location, and other determinants of wages, gay male workers earn at least 3 percent less than do otherwise identical men. Lesbians earn at least 3 percent more than do otherwise identical women. Previous studies for the United States tell a similar story. Do these pay differences reflect **discrimination** in favor of lesbians and against gays? Perhaps there is generalized discrimination in favor of "maleness," and stereotypical male traits are rewarded whether they are exhibited by men or by women. Lesbians earning more than other women may just reflect a broader kind of discrimination based on traits rather than gender.

> *Q: Given the results reported in this vignette, how do you think the earnings of bisexual men would differ from those of heterosexual men? Those of bisexual women from those of heterosexual women?*

17.13

Michael Lewis's book *Moneyball* (New York: Norton, 2003, p. 115) provides an excellent description of the economic costs of **discrimination** (in the context of choosing and recruiting young baseball players): "The inability to envision a certain kind of person doing a certain kind of thing because you've never seen someone who looks like him do it before is not just a vice. It's a luxury. What begins as a failure of the imagination ends as a market inefficiency: when you rule out an entire class of people from doing a job simply by their appearance, you are less likely to find the best person for the job." As with discrimination generally, anyone who does not indulge in this sort of discrimination and is willing to enlarge the set of choices from which people can be recruited may reap tremendous financial gains.

> *Q: Alan Greenspan, longtime head of the U.S. Federal Reserve, ran a very profitable consulting company before he took the Fed job. He hired only women economists, who unfortunately are generally paid less than men. His firm was very profitable. Why?*

Policy and Poverty

17.14

Deuteronomy 24:15 provides rules for the payment of workers: "In the same day thou shalt give him his hire; neither shall the sun go down on it, for he is poor." The legal requirement that a worker should be paid each day for the fruits of his labor is almost completely ignored in the United States and most developed countries today. Most workers are paid weekly, semimonthly, or monthly, even when their pay is computed on an hourly basis. Why the change? Partly the reason is that most workers have **long-term employment contracts** with their employers, so they know that they will be attached to the employer for a long time. Moreover, few workers in developed economies live hand-to-mouth. Most of them have enough savings in most cases from their earlier paychecks to tide them over to the next one. In a poor agricultural society, neither of these conditions holds. The workers are usually casual laborers, working for one landholder one day, another landholder the next. Workers also often had little or no savings, so that without the daily pay they, and their families, faced hunger.

> *Q: This is all true; but what would be the harm if people were still given their pay at the end of each day?*

17.15

In nearly every recession, Congress passes a law that extends unemployment benefits from twenty-six to thirty-nine weeks in many states as long as the United States stays in a recession. There is a real **trade-off** here. Making the benefits last longer helps maintain the spending of the unemployed, but the longer benefits give unemployed workers an incentive to stay unemployed. This is true whether we're in a recession or not. The argument for extension is that in a recession, the balance tilts more toward helping the unemployed because the incentive to remain unemployed matters little if few jobs are available. There's good statistical evidence that the disincentive to work generated by unemployment benefits is much smaller in recessions. Well and good, but the problem has always been how to turn off the spigot of unemployment benefits soon enough when the economy recovers to prevent them from making unemployment too attractive an option for people who would otherwise easily find jobs.

> *Q: If few jobs are available in the recession, why not allow people to draw unemployment benefits for fifty-two weeks? Or sixty-five weeks? Or until they find a job?*

17.16

The guy in the airplane seat next to me says he was fired from his job as a marketing vice president when his company was taken over by a European conglomerate. The new owner, like all employers contemplating firing long-term workers, did not want to indicate that the man's job was in jeopardy. If it had done so, the man might have quit while the company still wanted his services. A number of studies have shown that workers are generally surprised by plant closings and mass layoffs: Companies successfully hide information about impending firings. This man, though, had an inkling that his job was in trouble: Instead of printing up two boxes of business cards, the new company gave him only ten cards, and the cards didn't even have his job title printed on them.

> *Q: Why would a business not want to tell a worker that his or her job will end in one month? Why isn't the company better off if he or she quits now and the company avoids paying unemployment benefits and severance pay?*

17.17

Arlette Laguiller, a far-left candidate in a French presidential election, promised to push for a law banning layoffs in France. Who could object to this? Layoffs hurt workers and their families. But this law would have other effects, too. If employers can never lay off a worker, they know they will be stuck with unproductive workers when the **demand** for their products drops. To prevent this—and the likelihood of large losses in bad times—companies would be less likely to hire workers during good times. Instead, they would rely on a smaller workforce, just enough employees to keep a company profitable during bad times. They would have these few people work more overtime hours during good times. Madame Laguiller's idea would stop layoffs and reduce employment fluctuations. It would also reduce employment—the number of jobs in the economy.

> *Q: This legislation creates a **trade-off**: more jobs or more security for fewer workers. Which side of the trade-off do you prefer?*

17.18

Employers in many continental European countries offer much more job security to employees than their U.S. counterparts do. To overcome the inflexibility this creates, they also have vast numbers of employees on so-called fixed-term contracts, jobs that have a limited duration. These jobs are increasingly widespread; in Spain, for example, they now account for over 20 percent of employees. A new study shows the downside to these contracts: In Spain, such workers have substantially higher accident rates than do otherwise identical workers on permanent contracts, even newly hired permanent workers. Workers on fixed-term contracts don't expect to remain in the firm very long. With a short expected tenure, they have no incentive to invest in **human capital** in the form of the time and effort to learn safer methods of production. They also have incentives to cut corners in the hopes of demonstrating to the employer that they are productive enough to be one of the very few (currently, roughly 5 percent) fixed-contract employees who obtain a permanent job. Their higher accident rates are the unsurprising result of this combination of incentives.

> *Q: In light of this argument, what do you expect will happen to job accidents in a recession, when hiring is reduced?*

CHAPTER **18**

Public Goods, Externalities, and Property Rights

Public Goods

18.1

One of the teaching assistants pointed out a neat **free-rider** problem. A friend of hers was getting married. That was one of a number of weddings that took place in the church over a weekend. There was no time to put in new flowers before each wedding, so the brides were asked to chip in for the flowers. Several brides said no; those who said yes paid for the flowers (presumably the private benefit to each was large enough to exceed the flowers' cost), and the flowers were installed. The other brides paid nothing but had the free-rider benefit of the flowers.

> *Q: What could the individual brides have done to get the others to pay a "fair share" of the costs of the flowers? Is there any way the free-rider brides could have been compelled to pay?*

18.2

When we were little boys in the Chicago suburbs, one of our biggest thrills was throwing snowballs at passing cars. (A similar, but southern, example is reported by President Clinton in his book *My Life* [New York: Knopf, 2004]: He and boyhood friends would stand by a street throwing acorns at cars.) It took only one person to throw the snowball, but we all wound up giggling if it smashed into somebody's car window. We all benefited from the snowball throwing; and if more of us were in the group, each person would still benefit just as much—no one could be excluded. The snowball throwing was a **public good.** We all knew, however, that there was a risk that the offended driver would stop his car, run after us, and beat up the boy who threw the snowball. Only one person would bear the cost of throwing; however, that cost seemed so great that most times nobody wanted to throw the snowball. This public good was underprovided.

Q: What similar activities posed similar problems for you and your friends when you were little?

18.3

As I do before each midterm and final exam in an undergraduate class, I held what was supposed to be a one-and-a-half-hour question and answer (Q&A) session for my students this evening. This is not a review session: Unless the students have questions, I don't say anything. The problem is that most of the students arrived without questions, hoping that their fellow students would have questions prepared and that my answers would enlighten everyone. Each student relies on the others, hoping to reap the benefits of the **public good** that is created by my answers. But each student, not wishing to spend time making up questions, becomes a **free rider** on the other students. Today, this resulted in very few students bringing in questions. After fifty minutes and a lot of long pauses, I ended the Q&A session. I hope that the students remember what happened in this session when the Q&A for the final exam takes place. The public good problem in this case lasts over two periods of time. If the students realize the longer-term nature of the public good problem here, maybe they will be less interested in free riding off their fellow students next time.

Q: What, if any, are the incentives for the students to bring in more questions in the Q&A session before the final exam? Are they greater or less than the incentives were in the midterm Q&A session?

18.4

A tradition at the University of Michigan and a few Ivy League schools is the annual "Naked Mile," in which students run through campus naked to welcome the arrival of spring. At Michigan (where "spring" arrives late in April), participation in the Naked Mile has decreased sharply over the last few years. This is partly because the university has tried to discourage potential participants with warnings and also by arrests of some participants for indecent exposure. The real problem for the low turnout, however, is that the Naked Mile is a **public good.** Everyone can enjoy watching it without bearing the cost of participating—consumption is nonrival and the good is nonexcludable. As such, it is not surprising that the event creates a serious **free-rider** problem.

> *Q: What could the organizers of the Naked Mile do to encourage more people to participate?*

18.5

A neat example of a **public good** is a fireworks display. Nobody can be excluded from watching and enjoying it, and this leads to a **free-rider** problem. Moreover, there are **economies of scale** in producing it—the pleasures of watching a grand fireworks show are far greater than those produced by watching a few sparklers in your backyard. Both of these facts lead us to observe that the best fireworks displays are typically those produced by governments. It is rare that some other organization can deal with both of the problems, the public good problem and the economies of scale, that are entailed by the nearly unique characteristics of the production and consumption of fireworks displays.

> *Q: What about the idea of a city financing the fireworks by imposing a tax on those who watch the fireworks? Would that work?*

18.6

An Italian Boy Scout troop begins going on Sunday hikes, and the boys are told to ask their parents to pack them a picnic lunch. These are devoted parents and some pack fabulous lunches, but others just pack a small sandwich. The Scout leaders, seeing this, are very bothered by the lack of equality and insist that the boys put all their packed lunches in a big box. Each boy subsequently picks a lunch out of the box at random. No trading is allowed after the lunches are chosen from the box. Next week the parents again make lunches, but this time each one is tiny and contains very few goodies. This is no surprise: The Scout leaders have created a classic **public good** problem. An individual parent has no incentive to make a nice lunch, because he is almost certain that he is cooking for someone else's child. The lunch lottery creates an incentive for each parent to be a **free rider.** If the Scout leaders wanted to improve things a bit, they could let the boys trade after the lottery to get those goods they most prefer. Knowing that, the parents will try to pack lunches that are better—and they will try to include things that their own kid likes in particular but that other kids are not likely to want: If, like me, one boy likes peanut butter and mayonnaise sandwiches and nobody else does, his mom will make this, his favorite lunch, knowing that he will end up getting it in trade after the lottery. Allowing exchanges would reduce some of the public goods problem in this example.

Q: How does this vignette illustrate the issue of a **trade-off** *between* **equity** *and* **efficiency?**

18.7

During my two months of teaching in Moscow in 1993, I lived in a two-bedroom apartment owned by a former professor of the history of communism. The apartment, one of many in a sixteen-story apartment block, was immaculately clean inside. So, too, were the apartments of the neighbors who offered me tremendous hospitality (and copious amounts of vodka). The stairwell, however, was filthy, and the small lobby was filled with garbage, old newspapers, and dog poop. Why the difference between the apartments and the lobby? Simple: Each household was responsible for its own apartment, but nobody "owned" the lobby; the lobby was a common property resource not owned by anyone. No single household gained enough from keeping it clean to spend time and money cleaning it. The building hadn't yet been privatized, and the Russian government also had no interest in maintaining it. The only encouraging sign was that, near the end of my stay, the apartment "owners" had scheduled a meeting to devise some plan to clean up the common areas.

Q: Let's say the neighbors agreed to a schedule for keeping the lobby clean. Even with the agreement, how can they solve the **public good** *problem discussed here if nobody "owns" the lobby?*

18.8

Travis County is instituting an online jury registration process. Currently, when you are selected for jury duty, you have to go to the local convention center and spend an hour getting in the right line and specifying the times you can serve (or the reasons why you cannot). Every other Monday, about 1,000 people trek over to the convention center. With the new process, they can specify their availability and get assigned online. The annual cost to the county of setting up and maintaining this service is $300,000. Roughly 25,000 people will avoid spending the time doing this in person. It took me two hours the time I was called, so roughly 50,000 person-hours are spent each year. Let's say that registering online will take only a half hour; thus, about 38,000 person-hours will be saved. As long as people's time is valued at more than $8 per hour, this investment is justified. But the county must make the investment. No juryperson could afford to set up the online system on his or her own. This is about as close as we ever come to a new pure **public good.**

> *Q: If this public good were put to a vote—if there were a referendum on spending public funds on it—would you vote yes or no, and why?*

Externalities

18.9

A story on the Web this morning talks of the tremendous growth of pornography in rural areas. Apparently, national chains of porn stores have begun opening up at freeway interchanges, often occupying unused buildings that had been fast food or candy stores. Why the rush to rural areas? Cities have strict zoning requirements that are aimed at preventing **negative externalities** by imposing restrictions on the types of business that can locate in each block of the city. In many cities, pornography outlets are segregated in rundown industrial areas. Rural areas often lack these restrictions, with zoning restrictions, if they exist, treating all businesses alike. A new porn shop can easily open up in prime rural locations; **total fixed costs** in these areas are typically low, and there is also a large **demand** from truckers off the interstate highways.

> *Q: Could the federal government overcome the negative externality by outlawing pornography outlets with a quarter-mile of interchanges of interstate highways? Would this be a **Pareto improvement?***

18.10

A recent news story showed how complex the interactions that involve **externalities** can be. The overfishing of pollock in Alaskan waters has, so scientists claim, reduced the population of seals, which eat pollock. With fewer seals, orca whales have lost their favorite prey and have had to move closer to shore to prey on sea otters. The sea otter population is down, allowing their prey—sea urchins—to multiply rapidly and chew up the underwater kelp forests near the shore. Since the kelp forests aren't there, the shorelines are more exposed to waves that generate beach erosion and have caused an increasing loss of shoreline housing. (This chain is sort of like the children's verse "The House That Jack Built.") This six-step externality is the most complex I've heard of. It illustrates how something seemingly harmless—overfishing just one species—can generate serious negative effects in an area that to a layperson would seem very far removed from the action that originally produced the externality.

> *Q: List three remedies that the government could introduce to reduce the problem of beach erosion presented in this vignette. Discuss the total social costs presented by each of your solutions.*

18.11

I gave my final exam yesterday to 500 students in an auditorium that holds 850 people. Most of the students arrived on time and were seated when I handed out the tests. But about twenty-five trooped in late, anywhere from one to five minutes late. These latecomers imposed large **negative externalities** on their fellow students. They disturbed them as they walked down the aisles and, even worse, climbed over other students to find a seat. How can I reduce the externalities? I could simply ban the latecomers, but that seems harsh. I can't impose a monetary penalty, since the university doesn't allow that. Perhaps the best alternative is to make clear ahead of time that two points will be deducted from the test scores of all latecomers. If they know that ahead of time, perhaps they would adjust their behavior in response to this "tax" and reduce (to zero) the externalities they are imposing on the rest of the "society," which in this case is the other students.

> *Q: What if I just say at the end of the exam that I will be deducting two points from the scores of all students who arrived late? Would that solve the problem? Would it solve the problem if it is well known that I teach the same giant class every term?*

18.12

The Associated Press has a story about the **externalities** created by the rapid expansion of wireless and related devices. Many of these (newer cordless phones, "Bluetooth" wireless devices, and others) operate on the same radio frequency, 2.4 gigahertz. In a well-wired neighborhood of houses that are close together, one person using a cordless phone can, for example, disrupt her neighbor's home wireless computer network. To internalize this externality, one gentleman in the story has gotten a neighborhood group together to ensure that each household buys devices that operate on slightly different frequencies. His efforts show that the **negative externality** can be overcome, but that doing so creates costs in the form of the time spent coordinating different households' decisions about exactly what networks to install.

> *Q: What happens to the solution in this neighborhood if I adamantly refuse to buy anything but standard 2.4-gigahertz devices? How can the neighborhood group deal with me?*

18.13

I'm sitting in an all-day meeting in Washington with a bunch of other professors and federal civil servants. Suddenly, one of the professors gets up and starts pacing slowly around the room. He continues this off and on through the entire meeting. Assuming that he must be doing this to alleviate physical problems with his back, I ask him during a coffee break if his back is feeling better. He looks at me like I'm crazy, and finally says that pacing around the room helps him think better. He's maximizing his satisfaction (and presumably, too, his productivity); but the pacing is distracting to me and to other participants in the meeting. It has clearly generated **negative externalities** for the group as a whole. Whether the effect on the group's total productivity, both his and the rest of ours, is positive or negative is unclear.

> *Q: What could be done by the group to solve this externality problem at minimum cost to the group as whole?*

18.14

We awoke in the middle of the night and smelled skunk odor all over the house. I called the pest control company, and the guy came out to the house. He went under the house and showed us where he thought the skunk was living. He said that the best way to get rid of the skunk is to leave a bright light shining and a radio blaring overnight. (I call this the Manuel Noriega approach to animal removal, after the Panamanian president who was removed from office by the U.S. military and subjected to this treatment.) After a day, the hungry and thirsty skunk will run away and make his den elsewhere in the neighborhood. I apply the treatment, although I'm aware that I am creating a **negative externality** in the neighborhood: One of my lucky neighbors no doubt will find that the skunk has taken up residence under his or her house. At this point, however, we are very happy to impose these negative externalities on others.

*Q: The city government doesn't care about my skunk problem, and I don't want to pay extra to have the skunk taken out to the suburbs. Is there any way that my neighbors can get together efficiently so that I don't impose this **externality** on them?*

18.15

We were attending a wedding on an island just off the South Texas shore. The whole island is a development of expensive houses, most with boat docks. It was windy, and the wind was whipping the spray across the main road. I asked another wedding guest, one who lives in a nearby city, "What happens in a hurricane?" He laughed and said, "The houses are underwater, and there's lots of damage. But don't worry, the federal government helps the people get flood insurance." Federal **subsidies** may make sense to bail out people from unforeseen bad occurrences, but anyone locating on this island (and other islands and seaside locations) knows full well that he or she is prone to hurricane and storm flooding. Why should the average taxpayer subsidize flood insurance for this well-known risk? Worse still, the existence of subsidized flood insurance is a subsidy to construction along these coasts and, thus, encourages people to put up more buildings there than they would otherwise. It helps demolish wetlands and degrade the environment. Here is a case where the federal government creates a **negative externality,** as well as subsidizing people who are typically in the upper part of the income distribution, who are generally the only people who can afford beachfront and near-by property.

Q: Without abolishing this subsidized insurance, what would be the effect of a proposal to raise insurance rates in areas where substantial flood damage has occurred recently?

18.16

It's a Bad Externality That Does No Good. Two guys riding Harleys zoomed onto the freeway entrance in front of me at sixty miles per hour. They seemed to be likely candidates for death at an early age. I was depressed thinking about the prospect of their demise. No doubt they have families and, as the poet said, any man's death diminishes me. Also, their crazy driving increases the risk of my having an accident as I slam on the brakes to avoid them. There is a bright side that diminishes the **negative externality** that they are imposing on me and on the rest of society: They were not wearing helmets (which is suggested, but not re-quired, in Texas). This means that should they succeed in crash-ing, there is a strong possibility that they will be able to function as organ donors, helping to preserve the life of a desperately ill citizen with better sense than they have. Perhaps they recognize this silver lining in the cloud of their negative externality. Perhaps they rationalize their choice of not wearing a helmet both by the freedom they feel and the knowledge that they will do some good after death.

*Q: These motorcycle drivers create a **positive externality** in the form of the organs they eventually will donate. Do they create any other negative externalities?*

18.17

How Green Was My Windmill? One way to reduce the **negative externality** of air pollution caused when electricity is generated is to replace fossil fuels with windmills. In a number of areas, a large cluster of windmills can be an efficient alternative source of electric power. But do windmills really eliminate pollution? Probably not; while they do eliminate air pollution, they create visual pollution in areas where people value the unobstructed view of some particularly attractive natural or even man-made area. People on Nantucket Island off Cape Cod, Massachusetts, realize this and have been arguing against the creation of a forest of windmills just offshore. Similarly, in Ireland at the Giant's Causeway, a series of offshore rock formations that is one of the most frequently visited tourist sights in the country, a large protest movement has been launched against proposals to build windmills that would be visible when viewing the causeway. The negative externalities produced by electricity generation are not limited to air pollution.

Q: Wind generation is cheaper in those beautiful locations. How would you measure and weigh the benefits of putting the windmills there against the costs in terms of visual pollution?

18.18

It has been really cold in central Texas, which causes a problem for my wife and me each morning. We use sinks that face each other with a common wall between them. The same hot water pipe supplies the faucets in both sinks. Whoever washes first each morning must put up with two minutes of cold water before the hot water kicks in. This gives me an incentive to wash up second; that way she bears the cost of the cold water and confers a **positive externality** on me. If it were anyone else other than my wife, I'd probably be very careful to go second and be the beneficiary of the **externality.** But because I love my wife and behave **altruistically** toward her, I try to go first as often as I can. Love conquers even economics.

Q: What similar externalities exist in your household? Are you as altruistic toward the people there as I claim to be toward my wife?

18.19

One of my colleagues just returned from vacation in the Florida Keys. He was all excited that, at age forty-eight, he had gone scuba diving for the first time. He remarked that, unfortunately, the water was quite rough and made him somewhat seasick. He felt worse and worse, had to return to the boat, and eventually was so ill that he "fed his lunch to the fishes." He noted, however, that he had at least created a **positive externality:** His activity attracted a large number of exotic fish, allowing other divers standing on the boat much better viewing than they otherwise would have had. Although his seasickness was not a **Pareto improvement** compared to the situation if he hadn't been sick (he was made worse off), at least some other people were better off as a result.

> *Q: If you were a tour-boat operator and read this, what might you do to make the fish-viewing trip better for* all *of the people taking the trip?*

18.20

Out-of-state students at the University of Texas pay much higher tuition than do in-state students. But the extra tuition **revenues** are kept by the state of Texas, not by the university. University officials today said that they would like to have more out-of-state students (only 9 percent of undergraduates are not Texans), but why bother? The university doesn't retain the tuition revenues, and out-of-staters take places away from Texans. Despite these disincentives, officials argue that the presence of out-of-state students enriches the university experience for Texans, that the presence of out-of-staters on campus creates **positive externalities** for Texas students. Perhaps so, but is the value of this positive externality high enough to justify using scarce places on campus for these students? If the university were allowed to keep the extra tuition revenue these students generate—if it could internalize the monetary as well as the nonmonetary benefits—this positive externality might be worth capturing.

> *Q: If you were a state legislator from North Zulch, Texas, how would you react to the university's concerns? What if you were an alumnus of the university who no longer resided in Texas?*

18.21

In my office hours, I mentioned to a student that I pay my teaching assistants $5 each if someone gets 90 percent or more correct on the final exam. I had previously paid off only twice in twenty-nine years of teaching large introductory sections (total enrollment about 15,000 students over the years). The student pointed out very cleverly that any student who does well creates a **positive externality** (the dollars paid to the TAs), so students in the class should be subsidized to give them proper incentives to study hard. In fact, one student (the boyfriend of the woman who pointed this out) did get over 90 percent (sixty-seven correct out of seventy-two questions), even without the incentive. Think how many more students might have done this well with an incentive.

Q: Who should offer the subsidy, the teaching assistants or me?

18.22

I received a forwarded e-mail listing twenty-two supposedly clever pickup lines by economists for Valentine's Day. Some can't be repeated in polite society, but one polite one is, "Your presence is a big **positive externality.**" Now that is certainly possible, but one would hope that one's spouse or lover's presence is a big positive externality only for oneself. If he or she were a big positive externality for many other people, there would be a tremendous amount of fighting over the spouse or lover's affections.

*Q: List three real-world goods or activities that may represent a much bigger positive externality, or **negative externality** for one person than for anybody else.*

18.23

Over the years, some citizens have lobbied for the enactment of "takings" laws. These laws would require governments to compensate fully anyone whose property interests are harmed by government actions that generate **negative externalities.** Presumably, these efforts stem from a belief that compensation under rules of eminent domain—when government takes private property for public use—has been insufficient. Perhaps so, but to be fair the same people should also be pushing "givings" laws that would require those who benefit from the **positive externalities** arising from government decisions about land use to pay all their excess gains back in higher property taxes. Each landowner whose previously worthless property suddenly becomes a prime location for a motel or gas station when a highway interchange or airport is built should pay a tax equal to the amount by which the land has risen in value. If it makes sense to compensate for negative externalities, it makes sense to compensate for positive externalities, too.

> *Q: Is there any reason why it might be harder to measure the gains from the positive externalities than to measure the losses from the negative externalities?*

18.24

Grackles infesting Austin have become a year-round problem. They generate only **negative externalities:** They are noisy, they swoop by as one is walking, and their droppings in parking lots have created a tremendous demand for car washes in the city, thus helping waste scarce water supplies. They have no redeeming value. One might think the same would be true of the local bat colony. A half million of these flying mammals migrate from Mexico to Austin each spring, take up residence under a downtown bridge, and give birth to their pups. Unlike the grackles, their annual evening outings to hunt for food are a minor tourist attraction, and by preying on insects they help keep other pests under control. They generate substantial **positive externalities.**

> *Q: Think about nonnative animals and insects where you live. Which ones generate positive, and which ones negative, externalities?*

Transaction Costs

18.25

I'm in the habit of leaving the thermostat cover open if the thermostat is on "Hold" at a fixed temperature, rather than in its programmed cycle. My wife has now adopted this convention, also. We both now know that, when the door is open, someone has set the thermostat on "Hold." This makes it easier for us to know what's going on with the house and how warm or cool we can expect it to be. We have created an institution, the open thermostat cover, which reduces our **transaction costs.** We have created a rule that makes daily living easier and that economizes on our time. This simple household institution is like broader society-wide institutions: Much of their purpose is to generate certain expectations of members of society about how others will respond to various types of behavior. Institutions reduce the amount of time people need to devote to worrying about how others will be-have; this reduces time wasting and makes all members of society better off.

Q: What kinds of similar institutions have you set up in your dormitory, or your apartment, to reduce transactions costs? Did you set these up, or were they created by the university or apart-ment owner?

18.26

Fight at the Health Club Illustrates Transaction Costs. The health club limits the use of elliptical trainers to thirty minutes, and you cannot reserve them ahead of time. Two women sign up for elliptical trainers at the health club and then wait five minutes to get on them. They also reserve the ellipticals for forty-five minutes. Both of these practices violate the rules. Today, my wife got on the "reserved" machine and got into an argument with one of the women. The person running the club said it's OK for someone to sign-up for forty-five minutes if no one is waiting (even though signs say it's against the rules), so long as he or she gets off when asked by a person who is wait-ing. This imposes **transaction costs** on the person waiting rather than on the violator who claimed **property rights** on the machine by hogging it for forty-five minutes. Transaction costs matter a lot.

*Q: How can the health club make the person who is imposing the **negative externality**—hogging the machines—bear the costs of the **externality** generated by her bad behavior?*

18.27

A *Sex and the City* rerun has a scene where "Big" takes Carrie Bradshaw out to a fancy restaurant. Big lights up a cigar. The maitre d' comes over and tells him there is no smoking in the restaurant. The **property rights** to the air in the restaurant belong to nonsmokers. Big shrugs, continues smoking, then stands up and asks each of the other five diners if it's OK if he smokes. He also says that he is buying drinks for all five of them. They all say that his smoking is fine. Big has thus incurred the transaction cost of buying the property rights to the air in the restaurant. Since he's happier, and since the other diners agreed, his actions represent a **Pareto improvement** for the community of diners in this restaurant, at this point in time.

> *Q: What happens to Big's solution if every five minutes a new table of diners comes into the restaurant?*

18.28

Economists at Play. Nine of us have taken a jungle canopy tour this morning, and twelve other people are along. The tour is taking a long time, and we have to be at the dock to go on a sailing trip at 1:30 PM. Worse, the tour company promises a swim in a jungle pool after the canopy tour, something none of us economists wants to do. One economist suggests that we bribe the other people to give up their swim so that we can get back to town earlier. Another notes that because they have **property rights** to the swim—it was advertised as part of the tour—and know that we're in a hurry, they will overstate the amount they would require to give up their swim. Yet another economist points out that it's a shame that the swim was included in the tour, since the others could not have paid us enough for the swim to compensate for our impatience to get back to town. An initial grant of property rights has a tremendous impact on distribution. If there are **transaction costs,** as there are in this case, issues of bargaining and bluffing may prevent people from achieving a **Pareto optimum.**

> *Q: There were two buses taking the group. Is there any way that both the economists and the others could be made better off?*

18.29

A story on the Web announced that the town of Ridgefield, New Jersey, took a townwide "time-out" yesterday. All after-school, sports, and other activities were canceled, allowing families in this ritzy suburb a time for togetherness. Why is this necessary? Why can't each family take its own time-out? If one family doesn't participate, it loses out on the activity and in some ways falls behind others: The kids don't make the soccer team, Dad doesn't get the lead role in the Easter pageant, and Mom doesn't develop her softball skills. This is what economists call a coordination problem. The only way to get people to relax and get a bit less stressful leisure is to have some agreement imposed that ensures that people who don't participate in organized activities on that day do not lose out. The coordination required can't be created by one individual's decision, only by everyone agreeing, because some central authority requires it, to take it easy for some length of time.

Q: Is this the same as when a parent requires his or her child to take a time-out because the child had misbehaved? Why or why not?

CHAPTER 19

Taxes and Public Expenditures

Taxation

19.1

In the Beatles' song, the "Tax Man" sings, "There's one for you, nineteen for me." The Beatles are complaining about the high **marginal tax rate** that they faced in the United Kingdom in the 1960s. Implicitly, each extra pound that they earned left them only one shilling (one-twentieth of a pound in the old British money), with the remaining nineteen shillings going to the tax collector. This is clearly about the marginal tax rate, the tax on each extra bit of earnings, not the average tax rate, the ratio of taxes to total income. No tax system has an average tax rate of 95 percent on the entire tax base. The 95 percent marginal rate is also probably an exaggeration: Most systems have loopholes that allow some income to escape taxation when the rate is this steep. That Sir Paul McCartney is now a billionaire is pretty good evidence that the Beatles never really paid 95 percent of their earnings in taxes.

> *Q: What is the marginal tax rate on your earnings if you are working? What is your parent's (or parents') marginal tax rate? Are these the same as the average tax rates?*

19.2

A well-known economist published a scholarly article showing that there were fewer deaths late in December and more early in January in those years when the amount of tax on estates (assets left upon death) was lowered on January 1. Anecdote is not as good as statistical proof; but the death of my Dad's ninety-three-year-old uncle on January 2, 2004, made me a believer in the findings of this study. My great-uncle left an estate valued at $1.5 million. On January 1, the amount of an estate that escaped taxation rose from $1 million to $1.5 million. By living into 2004, he saved his heirs about $205,000 in taxes (41 percent times $1.5 million minus $1 million), as compared to the tax liability if he had died on December 31. With an initial **marginal tax rate** of over 40 percent, the extra two days mean a lot more for his heirs and a lot less for the taxman. Did my great-uncle consciously choose to live two days more to save us taxes? Probably not; but incentives do not have to be consciously perceived to affect behavior, in this case much to the benefit of his heirs.

Q: The estate tax is being phased out over through 2009. What do you expect this will do to the patterns of deaths that occur late in December and early in January?

19.3

A story in yesterday's *Wall Street Journal* talked about the new tax law that allows people who take the standard deduction on their income taxes to itemize their charitable contributions and deduct them from their Adjusted Gross Income (AGI). This gives low-income taxpayers, the people who generally use the standard deduction, a bigger tax break if they contributed to charities. Law professors don't like this, arguing that the standard deduction already accounts for charitable contributions. Economists say it wouldn't have much effect. The reason is that the price of a $1 charitable contribution is $[1 − t], where t is a household's **marginal tax rate.** Low-income households taking the standard deduction face a tax rate of only 0.15. The deduction wouldn't reduce the price of giving to charity very much for them.

*Q: Say the **price elasticity of demand** for giving to charity is 2. What is the impact on their charitable contributions if we make charitable contributions tax-deductible for low-income households facing a tax rate of 0.15?*

19.4

Until 1969, a visual artist could donate his or her work to a museum and could deduct the value of the work from his or her federal income tax liability, thus reducing income tax payments.

In 1969, this possibility was abolished by federal regulation. Not surprisingly, according to the *Wall Street Journal*, this change cut the number of works donated to New York's Museum of Modern Art by nearly 90 percent. This is fairly clear evidence that tax breaks matter to individuals' behavior. Congress is debating whether to reinstitute this deduction, in the hope of enhancing museums' ability to acquire art works. I would like to donate my grandchildren's artwork to a museum, state that it is valuable (which it is—to me), and claim the donation as a tax deduction. So safeguards are necessary: The museum should want the work, and the deduction should not exceed the appraised fair market value. With those safeguards, though, the deduction seems like a good way to induce a desirable change in behavior and to generate **positive externalities** in the form of more attractive art museums.

> *Q: Why might the government have abolished this tax deduction in 1969? Was it a purely stupid decision, or might there have been some reason for it?*

19.5

A legislator in California has proposed putting heavy taxes on soft drinks and candy bars. Her ostensible purpose is to discourage people from consuming products that contribute to obesity. She views obesity as a burden on the public, since it leads to more circulatory disease. The public interest, she would argue, requires this, since such disease imposes a **negative externality** on taxpayers who fund the state Medicaid systems that take care of many poor people's health problems. This is exactly the same argument that was used to justify the tobacco settlement, in which tobacco companies agreed in the late 1990s to compensate state governments. Here "compensation" will be paid by candy bar and soft drink addicts who continue to buy the products even after the prices rise in response to the imposition of the tax. Unfortunately, as is true with so many "sin" taxes, the **income elasticity of demand** for these goods is low: They are necessities. That means that the burden of the tax will fall heavily on lower-income consumers: The tax will be a **regressive tax.**

> *Q: How about instead arguing that dinners at any restaurant whose meals cost more than $30 per head are likely to be fatty and deserve to be curtailed. Would the effect on health be the same? Would the burden by income class be the same?*

19.6

The Internal Revenue Service ruled that spending for weight-loss activities is deductible from personal income taxes as a medical expense. By declaring this spending deductible, the IRS is allowing somebody with a 35 percent tax rate to have thirty-five cents of each dollar of spending at Weight Watchers, for example, subsidized by the federal government. Someone with a 15 percent tax rate has fifteen cents of each dollar subsidized. Because the U.S. income tax is a **progressive tax,** the **subsidy** is a bigger percentage gift to the rich than to the poor: The government is doing more to help the rich keep thin than to help the poor! The subsidy has other effects. It increases the demand for weight-loss services, helping companies like Weight Watchers. And people who are employed by Weight Watchers, such as Sarah Ferguson, Duchess of York, who advertises for them, are likely to see an increased demand for their services.

> *Q: The IRS does not allow people to deduct memberships in health clubs from their adjusted gross incomes in figuring their tax liability. How does this difference affect the demand for weight-loss programs relative to the demand for health clubs?*

19.7

Costa Rica, like many smaller countries, charges a departure tax at its international airport. I pay a $17 tax, but Costa Rican citizens pay $41, and resident noncitizens pay $61. Why charge foreigners less? The issue is tax competition. As a small country competing for business and tourists, Costa Rica can't charge a huge amount. If it did, travelers, knowing this, would go elsewhere. Its own citizens have little choice: This is the only way they can exit the country conveniently. Moreover, given the amount of tax evasion, a departure tax is a good way to collect taxes, and it is fairly **progressive:** Richer Costa Ricans fly out of the country more often than do their poorer fellow citizens. The $61 tax on residents must be demand-based **price discrimination** against people who have an even lower **price elasticity of demand** for departures than citizens do—probably wealthy foreigners who make their homes in Costa Rica but maintain other citizenship.

> *Q: Why not charge resident foreigners a $1,000 tax each time they depart the country?*

19.8

The state of Washington had imposed a licensing fee on cars that rose as a car's value increased. Fees on cars valued at more than $25,000 amounted to $600 per year. A referendum reduced this to a flat fee of $30 per car. Now, why would the average voter approve replacing a clearly **progressive tax** with a fixed-amount, obviously **regressive tax?** Either the average voter is dumb, not realizing that this hurts him or her and helps the rich, or he or she believes that cutting one tax will not lead to offsetting increases in other taxes. Appealing to the average person to help reduce a tax that hits mainly the rich is a common ploy. A good example is the pressure brought (successfully) on Congress several years ago to repeal a special excise tax on boats costing more than $30,000. The argument was that the tax hurt the workers in the boat-building industry. Possibly so, but it requires a strange theory of **tax incidence** for that to be true.

> *Q: If you had been in the state of Washington at that time, would you have voted to repeal the tax? How would the repeal have helped or hurt you, and how does that affect your opinion on the fee referendum?*

19.9

Several years ago, the state of Texas surprised the public by creating a tax holiday the weekend before school started. School supplies, kids' clothing, and related items were temporarily exempted from the 8 percent state sales tax. Who really benefited from the tax holiday? What was the **tax incidence** of this temporary tax cut? That depended on how the supply and demand for these items responded to the tax cut and the resulting drop in the net price. It's hard to believe that demand responded much because by that weekend many people had already bought the back-to-school items. If not, they had to buy them then—an **inelastic demand.** That would have led to a big drop in the net price: Consumers reaped most of the benefit from the tax holiday. Since then, the state has been offering this holiday annually, and most people expect it. They are adjusting their spending patterns accordingly so that now there is a more **elastic demand** on that weekend. Retail stores, too, can plan around this date all year long and be sure that they reap part of the gains from the temporary—but now fully anticipated—tax holiday. Buyers and sellers now share the incidence of the tax cut.

Q: If you want to make sure that consumers get the benefits of the tax cut—that the incidence is entirely on them—how can you design tax holidays to do this?

19.10

It's not often that the **incidence** of a tax is obviously split between producers and consumers, as the textbooks would suggest is the case. But on the day when the U.S. government reimposed a 10 percent tax on airline tickets, some of the airlines tried to increase fares by 10 percent. Others did not go along, however, and later in the day the companies dropped their fares to 4 percent above where they had been the day before (before the tax was reimposed). The fare increase settled at 4 percent. The consumer paid 40 percent of the new tax, and the producers paid 60 percent—even though the tax was imposed initially on the companies.

*Q: Draw a supply–demand graph in the market for airline tickets. Draw the **demand curve** in such a way that it generates a 4 percent increase in the **equilibrium price** after a 10 percent shift in supply. How must you draw the demand and supply curves to get this result?*

Government Programs

19.11

In introductory micro classes, we make the assumption that consumers maximize utility and firms maximize profits. What do governments maximize? This question has bothered economists and others for a long time, and attempts to answer it have led to one Nobel Prize in economics. One simple thought is that in their operations governments minimize costs. Another is that each regime in a democratic society reflects the will of the marginal (or median) voter, the person whose choice in the next election determines whether the incumbents or their opponents win. To me, both of these explanations seem even more oversimplified than our assumptions about maximization by firms or consumers; even a local government seems too diverse to have its behavior characterized this way. But we need some assumption to capture government behavior; just talking about it is not very useful.

> *Q: Others suggest that governments maximize the interests of the elected officials, subject to the constraint that the officials wish to be reelected. How might a government maximizing this way provide garbage collection services differently from one that tries to minimize costs? How about national defense?*

19.12

Newspapers are full of stories about companies that offer to locate in a state or city in exchange for tax breaks: no state corporate income taxes or local property taxes for an extended period of time. Others add direct **subsidies** in their requests to state and local governments. Perhaps the most visible claimants are professional sports franchises. Do these subsidies pay off for taxpayers? A reasonable criterion is that the discounted value of the extra taxes generated by the extra business and jobs created should at least equal the tax breaks and subsidies offered to the companies. I doubt that governments do much better than this breakeven level. The reason is that the companies and sports franchises behave like **monopolists** in bargaining with the various governments that are competing to get a company to locate in their city. As monopolists bargaining with competing governments, they can extract, in the form of tax breaks, every bit of **economic rent** that the locality might have gotten from the deal. Sports franchises do even better: Citizens seem willing to pay higher taxes or give up public services for the prestige of having a major-league sports franchise in the city.

> *Q: How would the amount of tax breaks that are offered change if the company was one that needed to use particular mineral resources that are located in only two places in the United States? Why does this outcome differ from the one described in the vignette?*

19.13

The state of California has enacted a law that will pay benefits to workers who stay home to take care of a sick relative. It will be financed by a tax on employers. What are some of the effects of these payments and the way they are financed? Let us view the world as having two kinds of companies, those with workers who will rarely use the benefits and those with workers who will use them a lot. The first kind of company has to pay the tax, but its workers get nothing. The second kind of company has workers who will get benefits paid both by itself and by other employers. The first kind of company is **subsidizing** the second kind. The **average total cost** of the first kind of company increases, while that of the second kind of company drops. The program will lead to an expansion of those companies that use workers with sick parents, kids, and spouses, and a contraction of companies whose workers have healthy relatives.

    Q: How could the tax be modified so that it doesn't affect average total costs differently among the various companies?

19.14

A headline in the Raleigh, North Carolina, *News and Observer* dealing with possible tax increases to finance higher education reads, "Mill workers making $25K must sacrifice to help faculty making $100K." The average faculty member in North Carolina makes less than $100K. The average taxpayer makes more than $25K, but probably does earn less than the average faculty member. The issue is not really taxpayers versus faculty members. It's taxpayers (who finance public higher education) versus the families of students enrolled in higher education. To the extent that students come from richer families than those of the average taxpayer, using tax dollars to finance public higher education represents a **regressive** transfer. If the **income elasticity of demand** for higher education is higher than the income elasticity of the state's tax base, raising tuition makes the burden of supporting higher education more **progressive**.

    Q: Assume that the income elasticity of demand for higher education is 2, a family with an income of $50,000 spends $3,000 on higher education, and state taxes are always 10 percent of income. How does the burden of higher education on a family making $50,000 compare with that on a family making $100,000?

19.15

While I was walking through the airport today with my parents and older son, as we passed Southwest Airlines, my mother remarked that she thought they were bankrupt. I said that to the contrary, they are the only airline that made a profit during the most recent quarter. My son said that I was wrong, and that Midway Airlines made a profit. I asked how that could be. He said that they were indeed bankrupt, were not operating at all during that time, and thus had no operating expenses. However, as part of the airline bailout they received federal funds this fall. It is impossible to defend this giveaway on any **efficiency** grounds. On **equity** grounds, unless one believes that the shareholders of this company are worthy recipients of a redistribution of funds from the general public, there is no defense either.

> *Q: What evidence would you need to support an argument that providing a bailout to Midway Airlines might be justifiable on equity grounds?*

19.16

The city government offers rebates to residents who purchase and install a new, more energy-efficient clothes-washing machine. The private company that supplies natural gas will add to the rebate if the washing machine uses water heated by a gas-fired, hot-water heater. The purpose of the **subsidies** is to encourage reduced energy usage. This offer is amazing: How many private companies would give you a subsidy to use less of their product? Although energy conservation is a fine goal, is this kind of subsidy, which requires customers to fill out paperwork and have a city inspection, the most efficient way to conserve natural resources? Why don't they just charge higher prices for natural gas? Why don't the city and state impose a tax on natural gas usage if they are serious about conservation? These alternatives would reduce energy use without wasting nonenergy resources: bureaucrats' and citizens' time.

> *Q: Assume that the **price elasticity of demand** for washing machines is 0.5. If the city offers a 10 percent subsidy, by how much will the number of washing machines sold increase?*

19.17

A great seat at the ballet in the gorgeous nineteenth-century Opera House in the center of Berlin, Germany, costs only $37—about one-third of what a seat of the same quality costs in New York. The difference between the **average total cost** and the ticket price is made up by **subsidies** from tax revenues from citizens in Berlin and from German citizens generally. The audience last night looked very prosperous, consisting of upper-middle-class Germans and a good number of well-off foreigners. Ballet and opera in Germany and elsewhere have a high **income elasticity of demand,** yet a large part of the cost is paid by taxes that are assessed on the average taxpayer. The subsidies must represent a **regressive** transfer, a shifting of resources from people around the middle of the income distribution toward those near the top.

Q: What would be wrong with the opera houses just doubling ticket prices?

19.18

Higher education spending by state and local governments was $9.97 per $1,000 of personal income in their states in fiscal year 1982, $8.24 per $1,000 in fiscal year 1992, and only $7.67 per $1,000 in fiscal year 2002. As income has gone up, government spending has failed to increase as rapidly, a result presumably determined by decisions of voters about how much governments should spend on this service. Although probably not an **inferior good,** public support of higher education is clearly a **necessity,** not a **luxury.** At the same time, we know that higher-income people spend proportionately more of their income on higher education; it is a luxury good at the personal level. Why the difference between the personal and the public? The marginal voter who determines how much is spent on this activity by the government must have a lower **income elasticity of demand** than the average person who chooses how much to spend out of his or her own income.

Q: Look around you in class and ask whether the typical student in your school comes from a family with income above or below the average in your state. (National average family income today is not much more than $50,000.) What does your answer tell you about the income elasticity of demand for higher education at your institution?

CHAPTER 20

International Economics

Comparative Advantage and Globalization

20.1

While I was checking in at American Airlines yesterday, the CEO of that company was in the airport shaking hands with employees. Amazing—the CEO of a major company spurring on the workers! The woman checking me in was less impressed. She remarked that she bet that he couldn't check me in. I didn't raise the question with her, but I wondered whether customers would want him to be able to do this. Aren't the company and its stockholders better off if each employee's **comparative advantage** is used—if it takes advantage of the gains to specialization? The CEO's time is better spent thinking about how to run the company more effectively, not learning how to do every job in the company.

> *Q: In some industries and activities, specialization makes more sense than it does in others. Describe the kinds of companies in which the comparative advantage of workers is more or less important.*

20.2

My wife and I needed to move 40 pieces of fencing, all with nails in them, from behind the house out to the street, and the nails had to be removed before the trash collectors would take the fencing. How to organize the task? There are three activities: dragging the wood, pounding the nails with a hammer so the heads stick up, and pulling the nails out with pliers. We figured that I have an **absolute advantage** in all three activities, but my wife probably had a **comparative advantage** in using the hammer. To minimize time spent on the activity, I dragged the wood, she hammered, and I plied. As the morning progressed, we each got faster at our tasks—our **production possibility frontiers** moved outward. By the end of the task, she may have developed an absolute advantage at hammering, so that our technological improvements increased each of our comparative advantages in the three tasks.

> *Q: Having developed our skills in these tasks, should we now go into business offering our services in removing fencing?*

20.3

I do most of the dinner cooking during the week. My wife is a better cook than I am, and she likes to cook more than I do. Also, my average earnings per hour worked exceed hers. So why am I cooking, if she has a **comparative advantage** in cooking, likes it better, and earns less on average per hour? The reason is that our decisions, like those of most people, are made based on **marginal,** not average considerations. Even though I earn more than she does, my time is quite flexible; I don't earn more by rigidly sticking to an 8 AM to 6 PM schedule. As an attorney, she needs to be in her office from 8 AM to 6 PM most days, so that the value of her time right before dinnertime is higher than mine. Our decision to have me cook dinner is a rational response to differences in the prices of our time at the margin. I cook because my time is less valuable than hers when the cooking must be done.

> *Q: Are there similar arrangements in your household, so that a person who might be less productive at a task does it because his or her value of time varies of the day or week?*

20.4

One of my pesky colleagues has mentioned several times that my Web site has "broken links," whatever that means. Apparently, the little pictures that people are supposed to click on are not there. He says it is simply a matter of adding two files. Now, I know nothing about this, so I asked our department's computer person to come to my office and take care of the problem. I told this to my colleague, who asked, "Why don't you do it yourself?" I told him that it's not my **absolute advantage** or my **comparative advantage.** I don't know how and don't want to spend time learning; that's why we have the computer consultant. The colleague said that I eventually would be doing this myself. He would be correct only if it takes me less time to do it than it would to ask the consultant to do it.

Q: What computer applications would you do yourself, and what would you ask for help on? How are these two types of activity different from each other?

20.5

Deans and the president are the big shots in a university. They are people the typical student never sees, but they run the institution. They usually come from the ranks of professors. Of course, preferences matter: Some professors who would be highly competent administrators prefer to keep teaching and doing research rather than becoming full-time managers, even though they would get paid more as managers. Many professors, though, enter teaching and research because they don't enjoy dealing with people and don't like being part of a hierarchy. They could not be managers. A few others may be better than their colleagues at research and teaching, too; they may have an **absolute advantage** at teaching and research. But they have greater interpersonal skills and may not be interested in continuing teaching and research. These interpersonal skills are rare among professors, and the few who have them become deans and presidents. Their **comparative advantage** leads them to fill these administrative jobs.

Q: Assume that one professor is mediocre at everything—teaching, research, and administration—while another is good at all these things. Which one should the university want to have as an administrator, and which one doing teaching and research?

20.6

Levi Strauss, the creator of blue jeans, is closing most of its remaining U.S. manufacturing plants, citing high labor costs in the United States for the fairly unskilled work. It will contract with other companies, mostly in developing countries, for manufacturing and will concentrate on design and marketing. Should we be depressed about this? No. It's a natural example of a process by which the United States produces those goods in which it has a **comparative advantage**—high-tech and innovative products—and lets lower-wage countries produce goods that do not require highly skilled labor. Yes. It's depressing that one of our most famous and oldest brands may not be produced here and that some very senior workers will lose their jobs. The hope is that our programs to compensate displaced workers—unemployment insurance and trade adjustment assistance (TAA)—will help these workers get retrained or at least ease their retirement. Indeed, TAA was designed partly to reduce political pressures against freer trade by people who might be harmed by increased foreign competition.

Q: How much compensation should the government give to workers who are displaced by foreign competition? If you ran the federal government, how much would you offer?

20.7

A fellow economist mentioned his eighteen- and fifteen-year-old daughters' unusual behavior. The older one, a freshman in college, brings her laundry home and expects the younger daughter to launder it. The younger daughter complies—but each time she keeps a piece of clothing that she likes most. Their father told this to the older sister, who laughed and said that's OK; when she comes home and her little sister is away she takes some of the little sister's clothing. Both sisters know all this, and both seem to view it as a way of trading. Like most trading that is voluntary, both sisters are better off. There are gains from trade in "stealing" each other's clothes!

Q: What will happen to the gains from this kind of trade as the sisters' preferences for the clothing they purchase become more similar?

20.8

The man in the next seat on a recent airplane trip starting chatting with me, found out I am an economist, and asked the following question: "I am a regional vice president for a large food-service company. We were just taken over by a huge British company that owns a variety of food-industry businesses. What is the net benefit of this internationalization for the U.S. economy?" It probably does not make very much difference for the U.S. economy. On the benefit side, the British firm bought his company because it believed it could run the company more efficiently. Presumably this will generate lower costs and, in this fairly competitive industry, lower prices to the American consumer. A negative effect might be that the profits from the American business, which previously might have generated purchasing power in the United States, will now go to British owners and raise purchasing power there. Perhaps a more important negative is that regional VPs might now see their career paths blocked unless they are willing to become more internationally oriented.

Q: List businesses for which this kind of merger would have larger effects on the U.S. economy. List some where the effects are likely to be even smaller.

20.9

Outsourcing is one of the hot issues in the **globalization** debate. Typically, outsourcing has been done in manufacturing industries or in low-level services. A story today talks about how churches are outsourcing religious services. Because of shortages of priests in North America and Europe, special masses (often in memory of people who died a while ago) are being outsourced to India, where priests are not in such short supply. This makes sense—the rationale is the same as for outsourcing generally: Produce the good or service where it can be produced most cheaply. So long as the customers (the people who want the final product or, in this case, who want the religious service offered) believe the quality is acceptable, they are better off having it outsourced than having it produced domestically—or in this case, not produced at all.

Q: Does outsourcing cause a loss of jobs in the United States in this example? Who is hurt by it?

20.10

A local "consumer advocate" is quoted in today's student newspaper: "To promote and support **globalization** is to be a selfish person and care nothing about the welfare of the world." No doubt she feels good saying this, but if globalization means rescuing workers, including very small children, from backbreaking low-productivity farm work and putting them into better-paying although still low-paid industrial work, it is she, not globalizers, who cares "nothing about the welfare of the world." She certainly doesn't care about consumers, American or other. If she did, she would recognize that producing goods for world markets in those countries where production is most efficient helps American consumers (and those of other countries, too).

> *Q: What is your reaction to a proposal to aid downtrodden foreign laborers by banning imports of goods produced by workers earning less than the U.S. **minimum wage**?*

20.11

The World Economic Forum, a meeting of government leaders, business leaders, and others, opens today. As in the past, it will be accompanied by protests by "anti-**globalization**" groups. I'm never sure what that term means. Is it less pollution, less cross-border ownership of assets, less international trade, or what? If it is less trade, particularly fewer imports, which seems to be the goal of the protests' U.S. trade union supporters, I am reminded of an old cartoon. The first picture shows a well-dressed family sitting around a table in a well-stocked kitchen, with the father saying, "We need to buy American." The second picture shows the same scene with Dad, Mom, and the kids naked; the pots, stove, and curtains missing; and almost nothing else left.

> *Q: Look around your dormitory room or apartment. Make a list of the items that would not be there if international trade were impossible. Ask yourself whether there are U.S.-made substitutes and how desirable they are compared to the imported items you own.*

Trade Policy

20.12

In 2002, President Bush went ahead and authorized **tariffs** on a large variety of imported steel products. Imports from Mexico and Canada were exempted. The reactions are completely predictable. The Europeans, Koreans, Brazilians, and Japanese are ready to complain to the World Trade Organization that the United States has acted unfairly. Those complaints take years to resolve, though, so they are also contemplating retaliatory tariffs on other U.S. products. The Germans even claimed that they let their own steel industry restructure, so why should they bear the cost of America's unwillingness to let its industry modernize? This kind of fighting is how trade wars get started. Without having to seem like a villain, Canada benefits from the Bush decision, because its steel exports to the United States have less competition. The Canadians can then sell more steel to America and sell it at higher prices. Small wonder that a Canadian official expressed approval of the U.S. actions.

Q: You are a typical citizen of a country that neither produces steel nor buys any steel from the United States. Does the new American tariff make you better or worse off, or does it have no effect on you?

20.13

U.S. candy producers are complaining that the high domestic price of sugar is forcing them to move production abroad, where they can buy sugar at the much lower world price. U.S. sugar growers are heavily protected, and the U.S. price is much higher than the world price, but that has been true for at least forty years. Equilibrium doesn't change unless some underlying factor has changed, so high sugar prices can't be the cause. What has changed is that **tariffs** on manufactured goods have been lowered fairly steadily, particularly within North America under the North American Free Trade Agreement (NAFTA). Since much of the imported candy comes from Canadian plants, lower tariffs (in the case of NAFTA, zero tariffs) seem like the cause of the relocation of candy plants. But the candy manufacturers are correct about one thing: Lowering domestic sugar prices to the world price would reduce the cost disadvantages of producing here and at least partly stem losses in domestic output.

Q: What would lowering U.S. sugar prices do to the market value of Canadian candy companies that are potential takeover targets by American firms?

20.14

International Trade and Technology in Action. The woman seated next to me on a plane to China works for a shoe company with headquarters in Dallas. The company doesn't manufacture shoes itself—it imports them from a factory near Canton, China. But the factory, which uses Chinese labor, is owned by a Taiwanese and HongKongese joint venture that supplied the capital and the technology to build the factory. With U.S. **tariffs** on men's shoes at 37 percent or below, it pays to use the inexpensive Chinese labor in what is not a highly skilled activity. The tariffs, the ability to gather capital and technology from different countries, and the knowledge and access of the Taiwanese and HongKongese to these markets have all combined to create an import that did not exist before 1990. Presumably the price of these shoes to the U.S. consumer is lower than from any domestic source—and the consumer is thus better off.

> *Q: Would the consumer be better off still if we helped U.S. shoe manufacturing plants by raising the tariff above 37 percent?*

20.15

The Economist has a story illustrating the folly of imposing **tariffs** in an industry where **average cost** varies across producers. The United States imposed tariffs averaging 27 percent on imports of lumber from Canada. You would think this would hurt Canadian lumber producers, and it did. But it also forced them to concentrate production in their most efficient mills, while the United States continued to try to produce at relatively inefficient mills. The result is that more U.S. mills have closed than Canadian ones. Not surprisingly, to limit competition still further the U.S. lumber industry would like to replace tariffs with **import quotas.** By limiting the amount imported from Canada, this would guarantee that the Canadians' continuing greater efficiency cannot give them an advantage over the increasingly relatively inefficient U.S. firms.

> *Q: Would the U.S. consumer be better off with these tariffs or with the quotas that U.S. lumber companies would like?*

20.16

In 1991, Colombia tried a new way of "protecting" its industries from foreign competition: It tried to auction off **import quotas.** Economists don't like import quotas. Unlike **tariffs,** which at least put customs receipts in the treasury's coffers, quotas restrict trade while earning taxpayers nothing. Auctioning quotas would seem to solve this problem, since the auction generates receipts for the government. Unfortunately, businesses did not want to bid on the import quotas, and they were undersubscribed. If businesses were perfectly certain about their demand for potential imports and if the red tape were minor, auctions would produce the same patterns of trade as tariffs. That companies didn't want to bid suggests that one or both of these preconditions weren't met. In any case, Colombia soon abandoned the idea and went back to tariffs.

Q: What are the characteristics of companies that are likely to bid more for the rights to import some product? Large or small companies? New or old companies?

20.17

Electricité de France, the heavily subsidized government-owned French power company, is trying to move into foreign markets, including that of Great Britain. The British government is complaining that this will represent unfair competition for its companies. Should average Britons be upset? Quite the contrary—they should welcome this. The competition will lower the prices they pay for electricity in two ways. The additional competition will force domestic firms to cut prices to compete. Also, to continue making profits in the face of lower prices, domestic firms will be forced to become more efficient through both better management and more innovation. The British consumer should be thanking the French public for its willingness to waste its funds by **subsidizing** a company that is willing to sell its power so cheaply so that British citizens may benefit.

Q: If you were an average French citizen, how would you feel about Electricité de France selling subsidized power in Britain? How would you feel if you were a worker in this company?

20.18

One of the most famous writings in economics is Frederic Bastiat's *Petition of the Candlemakers*, a spoof written in the 1800s in which the candlemakers petition the government to impose a **tariff** on their biggest competitor—the sun! Life apparently almost imitates art. American candlemakers have managed to persuade the federal government that Chinese candles are being **dumped** on the U.S. market. The U.S. manufacturers have a tremendous incentive to claim this: Under a recent change in federal regulations, penalties on foreign companies for dumping are paid to the American companies that sue successfully. Not only do the U.S. companies reduce competition; they also receive a subsidy from their foreign competitors. If I ran a company, I would prefer such an antidumping regulation to a tariff. Both help to insulate my product from foreign competition; but unlike tariff payments, which go into the federal Treasury, the fines for dumping go into the company's treasury!

> *Q: Other than the political power of domestic companies, is there any economic reason that might support letting the U.S. companies receive the penalties assessed on their foreign competitors?*

20.19

Today imports account for 90 percent of U.S. shrimp production. The U.S. Department of Commerce has approved protective tariffs against some shrimp imports in an **antidumping** case brought by U.S. shrimp producers. Domestic producers market fresh shrimp, while many of the imports are farm-raised, using cheap labor and inexpensive feeds. Not surprisingly, the **total cost** of imported shrimp is lower; but are the foreigners selling at a price below **average variable cost,** which is supposed to be the definition of dumping? I doubt it; they are selling a lower-quality product that the American market seems to want. The domestic producers are making complaints that are standard when a U.S. producer faces foreign competition. The domestic producers benefit from the tariff, and the federal bureaucracy has every incentive to enlarge itself by approving more such tariffs; thus, not surprisingly, these lawsuits succeed. What is sad is that the American consumer, who seems to be willing to consume lower-quality, but cheaper, farm-raised imports, must now face higher prices of those imports. The consumer will not be able to benefit from greater efficiency in domestic production that stiffer competition from imports might have generated.

> *Q: What if the United States just imposed tariffs on imports of farm-raised shrimp, leaving untaxed any imports of ocean-raised shrimp? Would that solve the U.S. producers' problems?*

Tips on Hunting for Economics Everywhere in Part 3

1. When someone postpones an activity, what does that imply about the rate of return on that activity compared to the cost of borrowing?
2. Ask yourself why people's wages differ and search for the underlying determinants. Look for differences by demographic group, skills, types of activities undertaken, and other potential sources.
3. Examine job hunting by people you know and consider why they accept or fail to accept jobs. What does their behavior imply about their attitudes toward work?
4. Look for cases where the activity of a person, firm, or company affects the well being of others in surprising ways. Look for public goods and free rides, and both positive and negative externalities.
5. Consider how outcomes differ depending on who has property rights. How do groups try to overcome initial grants of property rights? How do transaction costs affect these outcomes?
6. Watch for responses to changes in marginal tax rates, especially when the tax rate rises or falls sharply. Look at how behavior differs in response to changes in average and marginal rates.
7. Look for instances of the use of comparative advantage in your own activities and in changing patterns of international trade.

Glossary

Absolute advantage   Higher actual productivity than other producers.

Addiction   Increasing satisfaction from a good resulting from prior consumption of that good.

Altruism   Deriving satisfaction from increases in the satisfaction of someone else.

Antitrust   Policies or activities designed to limit monopoly or oligopoly power in a market.

Average fixed cost   Total fixed cost divided by the number of units produced.

Average product   The ratio of output to the quantity of an input.

Average tax rate   Total taxes divided by the total amount that is taxed.

Average total cost   Total cost (fixed plus variable) divided by the number of units produced.

Average variable cost   Total variable cost divided by the number of units produced.

Bilateral monopoly   A market relationship in which the seller has monopoly power and the buyer has monopsony power.

Change in demand   A shift in the amount people wish to buy at any given price; usually due to changes in income, prices of related goods, tastes, or market size.

Comparative advantage   Relatively greater productivity in an activity.

Compensating wage differential   Extra pay for an unpleasant aspect of an occupation.

Competitive equilibrium   A situation in a competitive market in which no firms have an incentive to enter or exit because there is no economic profit.

Complements   A pair of goods related so that when the price of one falls, the amount of the other sold rises.

Consumer demand   The quantity customers wish to buy.

Consumer surplus   The excess of the amount consumers are willing to pay for a good over its market price.

Demand curve   A downward-sloping relationship between quantity demanded and price along which income, prices of related goods, tastes, and market size are held constant.

Diminishing marginal productivity   Decreasing extra output as more units of a variable input are combined with fixed inputs.

Diminishing marginal utility   Decreasing extra satisfaction from each additional unit of a good or service consumed.

Discount rate   The extra fraction, D, required to make someone indifferent between having \$1 now and having \$$[1 + D]$ a year from now.

Discounting period   The amount of time in the future over which returns are received and discounted back to the present.

Discrimination   Treating objectively identical people differently.

Diseconomies of scale   Long-run average costs that increase as a firm increases output.

Dominant strategy   A strategy that is best no matter what the other party does.

Dumping   Selling in a foreign market below average variable cost.

Duopoly   A market with two sellers.

Economic profit   Revenue minus input costs (including opportunity cost).

Economic rent   The excess of the returns to an input above its opportunity cost.

Economies of scale   Long-run average cost that decreases as a firm increases output.

Efficiency   Using all resources and producing all goods in a way that minimizes cost and maximizes consumer surplus.

Elastic demand   Quantity demanded decreasing by more than 1 percent with each 1 percent rise in price.

Equilibrium price   The price that equates the demand and the supply for a good or service.

Equity   Fairness.

Externality   A cost or benefit conferred on others by the maximizing behavior of a person, firm, or government.

First-mover advantage   The gains in a game to the player who makes the first decision.

Fixed cost   Input cost that does not vary in the short run because it has already been incurred.

Free rider   Someone who benefits from a public good without paying for it.

General equilibrium   The equating of demand and supply in all markets at the same time.

Globalization   The expansion of trade and production across international borders.

Human capital   Skills and knowledge embodied in workers as a result of previous investments of time and goods.

Import quotas   Numerical limits on the amounts of particular goods allowed to be imported.

Income elasticity of demand   The percentage change in quantity purchased in response to a 1 percent increase in income.

Independence of irrelevant alternatives   The choice between a pair of alternatives is not altered by an offer of a third alternative that is inferior to one or both of the pair.

Inelastic demand   Quantity demanded decreasing by less than 1 percent with each 1 percent rise in price.

Inferior good   A good with a negative income elasticity of demand.

Labor theory of value   The idea that the value of a product is determined solely by the amount of labor used in producing it.

Long-run average cost   The minimum average cost of producing at a particular level of output if the firm plans to produce that amount forever.

Long-term employment contract   Relationship between an employer and employee that explicitly or implicitly binds them together for several periods of time.

Luxury   A good with an income elasticity of demand greater than 1.

Marginal cost   The change in total cost that occurs when output increases by one unit.

Marginal product   The change in total product that occurs when an input is increased by one unit.

Marginal revenue   The change in revenue that occurs when quantity sold increases by one unit.

Marginal revenue product   The change in revenue that occurs when an input is increased by one unit.

Marginal tax rate   The change in taxes when the amount taxed increases by one unit.

Marginal utility   The change in utility from a good when the amount consumed of that good increases by one unit.

Market demand curve   The sum at each price of the demand curves of all the individuals in the market.

Matching   Bringing together buyers and sellers so that they enter into a trade.

Minimum wage   A price floor on a wage rate.

Monopolist   The single seller of a good.

Monopolistic competition   A market characterized by many sellers of similar but not identical goods.

Monopoly   A market with only one seller.

Monopsony   A market with only one buyer.

Nash equilibrium   A strategic situation in which no side in a game has any incentive to alter its strategy.

Necessity   A good with an income elasticity of demand less than one but greater than zero.

Negative externality   A cost imposed on others by the maximizing behavior of a person, firm, or government.

Oligopolist   One of a small number of sellers in a market.

Oligopoly   A market characterized by few sellers.

On-the-job training   Investment in human capital through acquiring skills at work.

Opportunity cost   The value of an input, good, or service in its best alternative use.

Outsourcing   Buying goods or services from firms outside one's own economy.

Pareto-improving   A change that improves the well-being of at least one person without reducing anyone else's well-being.

Pareto-optimal   Not being able to improve the well-being of one person without reducing at least one other's well-being.

Payoff bimatrix   A matrix that shows the payoffs to each player under each combination of possible strategies in a game.

Positive externality   A benefit conferred on others by the maximizing behavior of a person, firm, or government.

Positive-sum game   A game in which the sum of the payoffs to the players is positive.

Present discounted value   The discounted value of a stream of future income or returns.

Price ceiling   An upper limit imposed on a market price.

Price discrimination   Charging different prices to buyers of a good or service.

Price elasticity of demand   The percentage change in quantity demanded when price rises by 1 percent.

Price floor   A lower limit imposed on a market price.

Prisoners' dilemma   A game in which both sides have incentives that lead them to an equilibrium inferior to a collusive equilibrium.

Producer surplus   The excess of the price received over the price for which a producer is willing to sell the good or service.

Product differentiation   Creating characteristics of products to distinguish them from other products and make their demand less elastic.

Production possibility frontier   A curve indicating a trade-off between two goods and showing the maximum combinations of them that can be produced with the available resources in an economy.

Profit-maximizing   Seeking the highest available difference between revenue and cost.

Progressive tax   A tax with an average tax rate that rises with the amount taxed.

Property rights   Control over a good, service, or set of rules.

Public good   A good whose consumption by one person does not reduce the amount available to be consumed by other people.

Regressive tax   A tax with an average tax rate that falls with the amount taxed.

Repeated game   A strategic interaction that occurs several times.

Revenue   Quantity times price.

Risk-averse   Preferring a choice with a higher chance of an average return to one with higher chances of large gains or large losses.

Shortage   An excess of demand over supply at the current price.

Short-run average total cost   The sum of fixed cost and variable cost divided by the quantity produced.

Speculation   Buying a product at one point in time, hopefully cheaply, and selling it at a later date, hopefully at a higher price.

Subgame perfect   A strategy in a dynamic game that yields the player the best outcome in all future periods.

Subsidy   An amount paid, typically by the government, to reduce the price consumers or firms must pay for a good, service, or productive input.

Substitutes   A pair of goods related so that when the price of one falls, the amount of the other that is sold falls.

Superior good   A good with a positive income elasticity of demand.

Superstars   People whose talents generate immense earnings.

Supply curve   An upward-sloping relationship between quantity supplied and price along which technology and input costs are held constant.

Surplus   An excess of supply over demand at the current price.

Tariff   A tax on an imported good or service.

Tax incidence   The share of a tax borne by each side in the market for the taxed good or service.

Tied sale   Requirement that a product supplied competitively be purchased together with a monopolized product.

Total cost   The sum of fixed cost and variable cost.

Trade-off   A choice between two goods or services that, because of scarcity, requires forgoing some of one to obtain more of the other.

Transaction costs   Costs of changing the ownership of property rights.

Unit-elastic demand   Quantity demanded decreasing by 1 percent with each 1 percent rise in price.

Utility   Satisfaction.

Variable cost   Input cost that changes as output changes.

Zero-sum game   A game in which one side's gain must equal the other side's loss.

Index